CONTENTS

Acknowledgements   iv
About the Authors   vi
Introduction: Navigating the River of Social Change   1

PART I: APPROACHING THE RIVER
1   Describing the River's Course: The Cycle of Social   14
      Movements and Your Organization
2   Power for the Journey: Power and Empowerment in   27
      Social Movements
3   Gathering the Rafting Party: The Social Milieu That   48
      Translates into Social Movements

PART II: FORTIFYING THE RAFT
4   Finding a Big Enough Raft: The Dilemma of Growth   58
      in the Group
5   Selecting the Raft for the Course: Choosing and Inventing   64
      Your Organizational Structure
6   Coordinating the Paddling: The Board of Directors   81
7   Recognizing and Sharing Leadership: Dealing with   95
      Issues of Authority and Control
8   Mapping the Journey: Incorporating Strategic Planning   106

PART III: STEERING THROUGH WHITE WATER
9   Creating Productive Meetings   118
10   Paddling at Our Best: Supervising Staff and Volunteers   129
11   Building High Morale: How to Develop and Maintain   144
      the Spirit of the Crew

PART IV: FACING THE BOULDERS
12   Developing Strength through Diversity: Diversity of   158
      Background Provides Needed Perspective and Energy
13   Dealing with Conflict   173
14   Balancing Demands of the Journey: Using Negotiating   188
      Skills
15   Pacing Yourself for the Journey: How to Avoid Burnout   195
      and Thrive while Working to Change the World

Epilogue   209
Index   210

ACKNOWLEDGEMENTS

GIVING LEADERSHIP TO ORGANIZATIONS IN CHANGING TIMES IS A LOT LIKE navigating a river in a raft. The pace of the river is sometimes slow and sometimes fast; the crew sometimes paddles together and sometimes boils with conflict; we sometimes see clearly how to avoid the boulders and sometimes—in a hostile political environment—we take our bumps.

This book grew out of a conference at Lake Sagamore in the Adirondacks of long-experienced leaders from around the United States, representing a diversity of causes and cultural backgrounds, from Lakota to Black Women's Health Project to white working class neighborhood organizing to gay/lesbian rights to new women's music to civil rights law to labor to peace.

The weeklong conference was sponsored by the Center for Change, a group of consultants and trainers who volunteer their time to assist grassroots organizations in becoming more effective. During the week, which was a combination of rest and recreation for tired leaders and a chance for them to network and share wisdom, consultants interviewed each organizer in depth assisting them in articulating the lessons of their long experience. Many of the quotes in the book come from the interviews, and summarize wisdom learned—often painfully, sometimes joyfully—from decades of work as activists. The authors of this book drew on this material as well as their own sense of what works and what doesn't work in growing more powerful organizations for justice.

The authors are grateful to the Lake Sagamore participants for their lively participation and their wisdom: Charlotte Bunch, Dottye Burt-Markowitz, Michael DiBerardinis, Ann Doley, David Fair, Judy Fairbanks, Emma Gonzales, Folami Gray, Jennifer Henderson, Joyce Hunter, David Kairys, Antje Mattheus, Bill Moyer, Torie Osborn, Beth

Grassroots and Nonprofit Leadership

A Guide for Organizations in Changing Times

Berit M. Lakey, George Lakey,
Rod Napier, Janice M. Robinson

Published in Cooperation with the Center for Change

NEW SOCIETY PUBLISHERS
Philadelphia, PA   Gabriola, BC

Inquiries regarding requests to reprint all or part of *Grassroots and Nonprofit Leadership: A Guide for Organizations in Changing Times* should be addressed to New Society Publishers, 4527 Springfield Avenue, Philadelphia, PA, 19143 USA or New Society Publishers, P.O. Box 189, Gabriola Island, B.C. V0R 1X0 Canada.

ISBN Hardcover   USA 0-86571-327-8   CAN 1-55092-274-2
ISBN Paperback   USA 0-86571-328-6   CAN 1-55092-275-0

We would like to thank those who have given permission for including excerpts from the following previously published material: *Strike* by Jeremy Brecher. Copyright © 1980, South End Press. *The Power of the People* by Robert Cooney and Helen Michalowski, eds. Copyright, ©1987, New Society Publishers. *The Truning Point* by Fritjof Capra. Copyright ©1981, by Fritjof Capra. Reprinted by permission os Simon & Schuster, Inc. *There Is a River: The Black Struggle for Freedom in America* by Vincernt Harding. Copyright ©1983, Harcourt Brace. *Organizing for Social Change: A Manual for Activists in the 1990s* by Kim Bobo, Jackie Kendall, and Steve Max. Copyright © 1994, Seven Locks Press.

Cover design by Margie Politzer. Book design by Pacific Edge. Printed on partially-recycled paper using soy-based ink by Capital City Press of Montpelier, Vermont.

To order directly from the publisher, add $3.00 to the price for the first copy, and $1.00 for each additional copy (plus GST in Canada). Send check or money order to:

In the United States: **In Canada:**
New Society Publishers   New Society Publishers
4527 Springfield Avenue   PO Box 189
Philadelphia, PA 19143   Gabriola Island, BC V0R 1X0

New Society Publishers is a project of the New Society Educational Foundation, a nonprofit, tax-exempt, public foundation in the United States, and of the Catalyst Education Society, a nonprofit society in Canada. Opinions expressed in this book do not necessarily represent positions of the New Society Educational Foundation, nor the Catalyst Education Society.

Rosales, Loretta Ross, and Barbara Smith. Two other important collaborators along the way were Betty Powell and Alicia Christian, who influenced our thinking in many ways. Still other activists have read and commented on various drafts and sections of the book. Of course, we authors remain solely responsible for the end product.

We deeply appreciate financial support from the Threshhold Foundation, Viki Laura List, and John Lapham. We also thank family and friends who encouraged us on what has turned out to be a very long project. For a book on teamwork, we have had a very good team.

ABOUT THE AUTHORS

BERIT M. LAKEY WAS BORN IN NORWAY AND CAME to the United States on a Fulbright college grant. In Philadelphia, she was director of Women Organized Against Rape and then directed Fellowship Commission, a human relations agency. Currently a Ph.D. candidate in organizational development, she is a freelance consultant and trainer who specializes in board development, diversity work, conflict resolution, and strategic planning.

GEORGE LAKEY GREW UP IN A WORKING CLASS family in an all-white Pennsylvania mining town and became a Quaker while in college. He has led organizations on neighborhood, city, state, national, and international levels, while writing five books on social change. A consultant and trainer, he has worked on five continents in settings ranging from boardroom to guerrilla encampment.

ROD NAPIER PH.D., GREW UP IN THE MIDWEST WITH Scottish and southern roots. After teaching high school and college students, he became a consultant and worked with a wide range of organizations, from churches to businesses; he has published six books on group dynamics and leadership. In 1986 he co-founded the Center for Change, which provides consulting services affordably to hundreds of nonprofit and activist organizations.

JANICE M. ROBINSON GREW UP IN HARLEM AND became a graduate psychiatric nurse. She joined the movement for community-based and controlled health facilities serving the poor and became executive director of a center in one of the most culturally diverse parts of New York City. She later moved to Washington, D.C. to direct the National Association of Community Health Centers. She added a Yale M.Div. to her RN and MA degrees and became one of the few African American women Episcopal priests. Washington-based, she adds consulting and training to her work as a priest.

THE CENTER FOR CHANGE (CFC), FOUNDED IN 1988, WAS ESTABLISHED TO promote justice, economic opportunity, environmental health, and social and political responsibility by consulting to profit and nonprofit organizations.

CFC works with a diverse and increasing number of clients who are asking the hard questions of society about government structures, citizenship, education, the enviornment and human services. CFC assists organizations in strengthening and enhancing their effectiveness by giving them the tools to lead and manage themselves.

The consultants are experts in areas of change management, organization development, leadership and community development. They represent a wide spectrum of racial and ethnic backgrounds. Within the Center, they are oganized into small, dynamic groups with special skills and talents covering a range of interests, such as education, community leadership, and managing diversity.

The forty consultants in the network are also established and nationally recognized in their own consulting practices. They work with organizations from grass root communities to corporations.

DEDICATION

To Christopher George Lakey, and all those millions of youngsters who deserve an environment that gives them the chance to thrive.

> *I was especially concerned to try to convey its long, continuous movement, flowing like a river, sometimes powerful, tumultuous, and roiling with life; at other times meandering and turgid, covered with the ice and snow of seemingly endless winters, all too often streaked and running with blood.*

> *...the river of black struggle is people, but it is also the hope, the movement, the transformative power that humans create and that create them, us, and makes them, us, new persons.*

—Vincent Harding
  There is a River: The Black Struggle for Freedom in America

Introduction

NAVIGATING THE RIVER OF SOCIAL CHANGE

SUDDENLY, THE WATER IS RUNNING FASTER. WE'RE PASSING MORE boulders; the river is narrowing and we're entering a channel. An island appears ahead of us and we need to decide whether to skirt it on the right or the left. We get caught on the edge of the island, then push off and keep whirling around while we're swept against another boulder, bouncing off to hurtle toward a waterfall that we can avoid only by paddling very, very hard and completely in synch. The adrenalin is really pumping now. That waterfall looks nasty. One of our gang was thrown out on the last one and it took forever to get her back into the raft. Paddle harder...*harder!*

Several of us are yelling now. Even though the words aren't clear it somehow helps. No! Our side stops paddling so we can swing to the left. It's too late. . . or is it? Our guide says paddle *now!* We make it! We make it, we miss the waterfall, we're here. And "here" keeps changing every second because the river, although slowing down, never stops.

We laugh and tease each other and mock complain that the water is now too smooth, while really we lean back and let the ache in our muscles subside. We revel in the delicious satisfaction and stretch like cats with the sun on our skin drying off the cold drops of water. And, like cats, we stay wary for the next patch where the river turns rough.

At times working for a better world has us coping with rapid and turbulent change, and at other times we do the work in a more stable environment. The authors have chosen the metaphor of a river's flow for several reasons: the dynamism of the river matches the dynamism of Western culture at the close of the milennium; the symbol of the river resonates deeply in the cultures of African Americans and others

1

who have struggled long for justice; and the persistence of the river gives us the perspective not of controllers but of navigators, who use our wits and our unity to get safely through.

The metaphor of the river organizes the book, and the experience of this blue-collar peace activist inspires the book with its practicality:

My father's life was hard. There was never enough money for the family, he was looked down on for being blue collar, he didn't fit into my mother's church, he had dead-end jobs. I remember his good days, though. Some of them were when he solved something that was puzzling him, a new way of doing something at work, or a different way of gardening. Then he'd get excited, and feel in charge of things. It's not that his life would get easy. But there was a different flavor then, like he saw his own power to turn things in some way and he'd lighten up. At those times it was like his life changed from being a burden to being a challenge.

The father of the man who told us this story knew something all of us can use: turning burdens into challenges enables us to lighten up. Easier said than done? The activist said his dad did that when he'd puzzle something out, try a new way, or find a new angle. Whether rafting a rough river with a group or handling life's responsibilities as an individual, it's clear that our experience gets better when we see living and working as a challenge, something we can rise to. Finding new angles on how to do it makes it more rewarding.

This book is about using teamwork to build and maintain effective organizations. The authors know personally how hard this is to do. One of us spent many years assisting people in a low-income, African American community to fight the system instead of each other; they succeeded in building and running a community health center. One of us worked with women who'd been raped, supporting them to stand up for themselves personally and to build a political force for increasing women's power. One spent countless hours with educators, coaching them to see how the needs of thirsty minds could be met with open, dynamic learning models rather than pedagogical systems of control. One built an alliance of people of color and whites, unions and middle class idealists, and people who focus on national policy and those who focus on neighborhood issues. We all have days when the challenge simply seems too great: how to maintain high productivity, while working in a way that is accountable, consistent with our values, and innovative!

Activist leaders often face this challenge with minimal affirmation and few people around us acknowledging how hard we work and how much we care. Unconstructive criticism and attacks from our own ranks are like sand in our gears. The larger culture, furthermore, is often hostile or indifferent; the media usually reflect that by trivializing or ignoring our work. Many of us are also perfectionists who carry inside our heads a highly self-critical voice. Even when others are pleased with how things are going at the moment, this nagging voice manages to point out what may not be good enough.

> **Recognize that what you are doing is difficult, not just that you aren't working hard enough or you are not smart enough. It is difficult.**
>
> —*a long-time, Irish American labor organizer*

This book is about working for a better world, for social change. At times this is dirty, gritty and unrewarding. This book doesn't pretend that social change work is made easy by a few formulas and a positive attitude. Activists can, though, like the father in the story, find a hard vocation made a bit easier when we get interested in the process, finding some new angles. We'll get better results and like the whitewater rafters, we can even find exhilaration in the adventure of social change when we have a high-morale group, good guidance, and a good map.

African American historian Vincent Harding's use of the river as a metaphor for social change, quoted just before this introduction, provides guidance. Sometimes the river flows slower, and sometimes faster. The slower times are good times to practice our paddling skills, because when we hit white water we have all we can do to guide our boat between rocks and treacherous whirlpools.[1] Some systems theorists have lately been developing "chaos theory" to describe the amazingly rapid change that systems sometimes go through.[2] This book is for people who want organizations which can actively participate and be useful in chaotic situations without themselves disintegrating.

This book is for you if
- you care passionately about service and creating a just society,
- you feel there's "not enough": time, money, competency, volunteers, staff, leadership, sense of direction,
- you don't want to read a lot of complex theory to get to practical ideas for bettering your organization,
- you do want practical ideas that are backed by years of activist experience and the latest in social science theory,
- you don't mind being challenged in some assumptions and habits you may now have.

This book is not for you if
- you want an organizer's manual for campaigning and mobilizing people,
- you want comparative approaches to neighborhood organizing, union organizing, etc.

You will find material here useful for campaigning and mobilizing people, but the focus of the book is on the health of the organization itself.[3]

This book may be useful to your organization if
- the staff is risking burnout,
- there are ego-games and bickering over power and status,
- the board of directors is passive or overly involved,
- there's a lack of diversity,
- your program is driven by events with no strategic plan,
- boring meetings take away people's motivation to come,
- conflicts over strategy and policy don't get resolved,
- volunteers turn over too rapidly,
- morale is not as high as it could be.

What we offer in this book is a set of techniques that are tested by experience. They don't always work everywhere—you have to decide which may fit your unique situation, and you may take some and adapt them in some way. One of the experienced organizers we interviewed, an African American woman organizing in poor neighborhoods, commented: "Techniques empower you. Have the courage to try them and the belief that they work....Know that sometime you won't have to use the techniques as a walking stick because you will believe that you have the power."

To supplement our own experience and study, the authors interviewed dozens of veteran activists who are leaders in their fields. These organizers work with a broad range of people in struggle. The result is not simply a collection of techniques, as important as that is.

The book also reflects a way of thinking about organization: a perspective which enables the reader to become proactive, to see tensions before they become crises, to make the most out of the crises that do show up, and to maintain a sense of balance and power.

Levels to Think about in Working for Social Change

Social change is easier to work for than to define. When we use the term, we mean intentional steps that move society in the direction of equality, support for diversity, economic justice, participatory democracy, environmental harmony, and waging and resolving conflicts nonviolently. It's useful to think of four levels that influence each other as we work for change: the individual, the organization, the social movement, and society.

> **It's difficult to teach people—movements tend to repeat stages rather than learn from the past. They have to experience certain processes to learn that the injustice won't be corrected just because it's wrong. Frame demands and think out strategies with a long-term view—educate on a deeper level. Have patience, knowing we have to go through stages may help us be more patient.**
>
> —*an East Coast man with long experience organizing in the gay community*

5

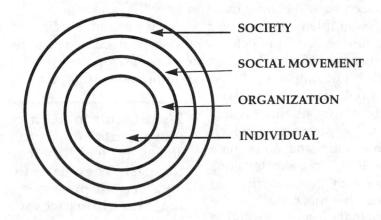

The individual is what we mostly see in our organizations, so there seems no risk of forgetting this level. Wrong! In the rush of deadlines and the pressure of crises, the nurturing of the intelligence and inner strength of individuals in the organization can be overlooked. We can forget that without healthy individuals to perform the organizational roles the organization itself gets sick.[4] Fortunately, younger activists increasingly are exploring connections between politics and spirituality and being open about those connections.

The organization is a cluster of roles held together by coordination and a mission; typical roles are "volunteer," "program staff," "board member," "contributor," etc. Individuals can enter and leave the roles while the organization remains stable, declines, or grows. Structurally, an organization needs roles, coordination, and mission. This book is mostly about the organizational level.

An organization doesn't exist in a vacuum, of course. It operates in an environment of social movements—citizen efforts to change conditions, policies, or structures by joining together and campaigning. The organization may be an expression of a social movement: the Southern Christian Leadership Conference was organized by African Americans in the South who were marching and boycotting buses in the 1950s. The organization may, on the other hand, be engaged in nurturing and supporting a movement: the American Friends Service Committee supported the California farm workers in creating their movement led by Cesar Chavez.[5] Even an agency that sees advocacy for change as only a part of their mission—a group that mainly provides services to people with AIDS, for example—is influenced one way or another by its social movement environment.

Movements grow, peak, decline, revive, and die in a larger environment we call society. Movements are enormously influenced by larger social, economic, and cultural forces. It's no accident, for example, that the civil rights movement of the 1950s and 1960s was so frequently led by clergy. A study by one of the authors found that, among African Americans in the South, economic changes and urbanization were resulting in a new trend: other professionals were taking more and more leadership in communities where clergy had previously been by far the most influential. Their community leadership no longer unchallenged, it became very much in the interest of black clergy to act to regain their traditional leadership role, even though that often meant new behaviors and the use of new techniques, such as civil disobedience. They legitimized these new behaviors by reinterpreting the Gospel, changing it from a source of consolation for the condition of oppression to a source of motivation for struggle against oppression. Jesus became, in this new interpretation, "the first freedom rider." This is not to say that all or even most African American clergy gave leadership in the freedom movement. However, to understand the participation of so many ministers who did act as leaders, given the quietist role they generally played before, it helps to see the wider trends.

What this means is that a southern activist of the early 1950s, who might be disgusted by insufficiently militant leadership among clergy, would have been mistaken to write off the potential simply on the grounds of the past or with a shrug about religion being the opiate of the masses. Keeping the bigger picture of societal trends in mind can increase our openness to powerful possibilities.

What key features of the larger landscape are influencing social movements now? Our list would include changing technology, global economic reorganization, the collapse of communism as an anchoring ideology for the left, and the drive of identity groups for priority attention.

Many observers are arguing that the economy is no longer led by industry, but by electronics, a shift which might be as fundamental as the earlier change from agriculture to industry.[6] This has tremendous implications for us as organizers: How will people make their living? At what wages? If they have to work two jobs or longer hours, will they be available to fight for justice? Will they stay in one place or move frequently? Will the number of structurally unemployed continue to grow? If so, what social roots will stabilize them enough to be able to stick together to demand change? Will professionals continue to experience little time for community participation?

Very big decisions about the future are being made without economic democracy. This is not new. Corporate links with government have cost the people for a long time. In Canada, for example, large corporations persuaded the government to give back an estimated $2.5 billion as tax incentives for four years of job-creating investments; the investments in turn amounted to an estimated $846 million.[7] The trend is to reduce the level of public influence that did exist, in the name of deregulation. Decisions about the new order are either left to "market forces" or made by corporate chiefs. Chief executive officers are required to do what is best for their own corporations, even if it hurts society and the environment. The North American Free Trade Agreement (NAFTA), for example, gives even more permission for corporations to juggle currency, pollution, credits, labor supply, production sites, and taxes from one nation to another, mixing and matching to boost the bottom line, leaving communities in ever greater jeopardy.

Communism as a state ideology has been an anchoring point for many people on the left, even those who have never been Leninists and who have fiercely denounced the Soviet empire as a tyranny. Communism was a large-scale alternative to capitalism, and however monstrous it was for democratic socialists, it nevertheless implied that it might be possible to create alternatives: humanity is not fated to suffer from capitalism without relief. When corporations propped up dictatorships, devastated the environment, and threw people out of work, activists could believe humanity has a capacity to create alternative, large-scale economic and political systems that give hope for a better way. That belief is now melting like snow in the summer. Even the democrat's comfort in saying "I told you so" in the face of continuing revelations of communist blunders and betrayals, is a cold

8

comfort if it leaves the world to the unchallenged hegemony of the rich.

One implication for organizers is a temptation to think small, to settle for micro-changes. The challenge will be to dare people to think boldly, to envision transformative change. Another implication is that the right wing has lost its major enemy and fundraising appeal—the "evil empire" and its ideology. The right's attacks on homosexuals, in a quest for a new enemy to unify its ranks, has serious implications for organizations.

Identity groups are coming on stronger as the century draws to a close. Sociologist Elise Boulding points out that the leading assumption in the first half of this century was that nation-states would become melting pots, where people would gradually give up their ethnic and other group identities to wear proudly the label of citizen. Enormous energy was given to back that assumption, even to the point of forbidding the use of minority languages in schools. What we now call cultural genocide has been largely a failure. The 10,000 societies on earth have stubbornly refused to break down into individual citizens of the 184 nation-states.[8] What's more, identity groups have been proliferating beyond the 10,000 ethnically-defined societies to include gender, sexuality, physical difference, age, and so on. To the disappointment of Marxists who wanted these identities to submerge into class membership, as well as capitalists who wanted the role of citizen to rule the day, identity groups increasingly are claiming a priority place. This has enormous implications for organizational life; corporations and nonprofits alike are trying to make up for lost time by hiring consultants to run diversity workshops.

Changing technology and economic organization, the collapse of state-sponsored communism, and the assertiveness of identity groups are dramatically changing the terrain through which the river runs. Wise organizers will support members in dealing with the disorientation of such dramatic shifts, and in experimenting for themselves with inner work for finding equilibrium.

Journeying on the River: How This Guidebook Works

Even though our focus is on organization, the other three levels—society, social movement, and individual—are addressed in this book.

In Part I, "Approaching the River," we first describe the dynamics of how social movements develop over time. We then clarify what kinds of power we'll need for the journey. The societal conditions that facilitate the emergence of social movements influence who joins them, and on what terms; leaders therefore need to make informed decisions on how to recruit members.

Having looked at the societal and social movement levels, we are ready for the organizational level. Using our river metaphor, it's time for Part II, "Fortifying the Raft"—the infrastructure of the organization. First we need to find a big enough raft, because as organizations grow beyond the initial founding circle, dynamics occur that can bring a lot of alienation if not handled well. We also need to choose a structure that makes sense for a growing organization, or for an organization that is stabilizing after a period of growth.

Trying to run a river without coordination of the rafters is inviting disaster. In chapter six we share advice on the governance structure of the organization, its board of directors, coordinating committee, or staff collective. Formal structures can break down under the stress of white water if there is insufficient experience in dealing with issues of authority and control, and so we discuss recognizing and sharing leadership.

When the right size and character of the raft is chosen, coordination of paddling is agreed on, and leadership issues are confronted, the group is ready to map the journey: to create a flexible, strategic plan for making this a more just world.

Having a clear structure in place with a strategic plan complete with projected action steps (Part II), still does not amount to a whole lot if the organization cannot follow through. Part III, "Steering through the White Water," is about management issues useful for the more routine, as well as the more exciting, times.

Week in and week out, management happens through nurturing and coaching members; the main mechanisms are meetings and supervision. In chapter nine we describe the art of meeting facilitation as a kind of guidance function. The facilitator doesn't paddle the raft by him or herself, but guides the process. The supervision chapter explains how to coach staff and volunteers to get consistently strong work.

High morale is not accidental, whether in a raft or in an organization. We've distilled from the experience of veteran organizers specific tips on how to improve morale in chapter eleven.

In Part IV, "Facing the Boulders," we learn how to adjust and change as the river throws up fresh challenges. In chapter twelve, the organization develops its strength through diversity. In chapter thirteen, with the inevitable conflicts in the team rising to the surface, a whole set of principles are outlined on how to turn conflicts into growth for the organization.

How do individuals thrive on this river journey? After many chapters spotlighting the organizational team, the last two chapters address the individual rafter. As important as the teamwork is in the middle of the rapids, each individual still needs to maintain her or his own balance. We outline specific skills in negotiation in chapter fourteen. In chapter fifteen we share action-tested ways to avoid burnout and tools the individual can use to thrive in the uncertainties of work in nonprofit and grassroots organizations.

The final word in this chapter goes to another long-time African American woman organizer. Her advice underlies the whole book.

"Patience is extremely important—listening to what other people have to say. Know your history, understand the movement you're working in, understand the human process that people who are oppressed go through."

Notes

1. The metaphor of the white water is used by Peter B. Vaill in his book *Managing as a Performing Art: New Ideas for a World of Chaotic Change* (San Francisco: Jossey-Bass, 1989). We came up with it independently, and recommend his book for another perspective on organizational leadership.
2. See, for example, organizational consultant Margaret J. Wheatley's book *Leadership and the New Science* (San Francisco: Berrett-Koehler Publishers, 1992).
3. Manuals for campaigning and mobilizing people include: Kim Bobo, Jackie Kendall, and Steve Max, *Organizing for Social Change* (Washington: Seven Locks Press, 1991); Si Kahn, *Organizing: A Guide for Grassroots Leaders* (New York: McGraw-Hill, 1981); Bill Lee, *Pragmatics of Community Organization* (Mississauga, Ont.: Commonact Press, 1986); Ed Hedemann, ed., *War Resisters League Organizer's Manual* (New York: War Resisters League, 1981); Katrina Shields, *In the Tiger's Mouth: An Empowerment Guide for Social Action* (Philadelphia and Gabriola Island, BC: New Society Publishers, 1994), Lee Staples, *Roots to Power: A Manual for Grassroots Organizing* (New York: Praeger, 1984).
4. Connections between individual and organizational pathology are explored by Anne Wilson Schaef and Diane Fassel in *The Addictive Organization* (San Francisco: Harper, 1988).
5. Sociologist Aldon D. Morris calls organizations whose mission is to nurture social movements, "movement halfway houses." See *The Origins of the Civil Rights Movement* (New York: The Free Press, 1984).
6. Futurist Alvin Toffler puts the argument clearly in *The Third Wave* (New York: Bantam Books, 1984).
7. Cited by Professor Bill Lee at the McMaster University School of Social Work; see his book *Pragmatics of Community Organization*, 2nd ed. (Mississauga, Ont.: Commonact Press, 1992), p. 25.
8. Elise Boulding, personal communication. See her book *Building a Global Civic Culture: Education for an Interdependent World* (New York: Columbia University Teachers College Press, 1988).

PART I

APPROACHING THE RIVER

The internal life of an organization is enormously influenced by what's around it—the ebb and flow of social forces, the river of history. In Part I we explore how the cycle of social movements influences participation, the several faces of power, and how groups can relate more effectively to potential members.

Chapter 1

DESCRIBING THE RIVER'S COURSE

The Cycle of Social Movements and Your Organization

ONE OF THE HARDEST TASKS IN SOCIAL CHANGE IS FIGURING OUT
where we are on the journey to our goals. Typically, our
organization is chaotic and we work day-to-day to solve problems
like cash flow, erratic volunteers, political differences. Maybe
we're farther ahead than a year ago, but then again, maybe not.
It's a good time for a map which describes the river's course. The
map we've found useful is one which puts our organizations in
their context of social movements.

In our reading of history, it takes a social movement to make
major changes. Social agencies, expert commissions, courts, and
professional advocates can sometimes achieve smaller changes or
open the door a crack to let some individuals get new
opportunities. When advocates intervene without a movement,
however, they usually just succeed in shifting some costs of
oppression from one group to another, or even one person to
another. For example, it is usually convenient in a capitalist
economy to maintain unemployment in order to keep labor costs
down. (When workers compete with each other for scarce jobs,
wages stay low: it's the law of supply and demand.) Economic
policy under capitalism is usually, therefore, to maintain high
unemployment rates. Advocates whose program is job training, in
that context, are intervening to give those they train an edge for the
scarce supply of jobs over those who are untrained. The countries

14

which have created systems for handling unemployment—Sweden, for example—did so after social movements forced a shift in economic policy.[1]

History includes many examples of social movements forcing a change which was resisted by powerholders. Here are some:

- independence from Britain
- freedom of religion
- abolition of slavery
- woman suffrage
- child labor laws
- the eight-hour day
- desegregation of public facilities
- voting rights for African Americans
- unions for workers
- civil rights ordinances for lesbians and gay men

It is not only necessary to build social movements to get change, but also desirable. No one, not even the most charismatic leader or the wisest expert, can truly give another the experience of freedom. Empowerment only happens when oppressed people participate in their own liberation.

Oppression is not just a matter of external coercion and discrimination, like police brutality or poor schools in poor neighborhoods. The institutions of domination send messages which justify oppression: "working class people are dumb," "blacks are lazy," "Asians are sly," "Jews are stingy," etc. Sadly, these messages are internalized by individuals in the oppressed group and play havoc with their self-esteem, resulting in the false belief that people don't really deserve just and equal treatment.

This process of weakening self-esteem is known as internalized oppression. It's easy to observe in young people who, as they get older and hear these oppressive messages repeated over and over in the media, school, and home, lose their confidence and replace it with hanging back or with a kind of defensive bravado. One of the early contributions of the women's movement was to develop assertiveness training as a way of rebuilding the confidence of women conditioned into passive-aggressive kinds of behavior.[2]

Internalized oppression undermines the ability of people to stand up for themselves. It also conditions people to attack each other within their group. Leaders are particular targets. The attacks may take different forms for different groups: women may engage in malicious gossip, blacks "read" each other, boys call each other sissies. Leaders may be the object of destructive criticism or sarcastic behind-the-back jokes. A healthy trend among gay activists is increasing challenge to the history of "eating our leaders." On the organizational level, unions raid each other for members and leftist groups publically attack each others' intelligence and integrity.

Internalized oppression is also destructive of coalition-building, because people suffering from low self-esteem take it out on groups suffering from other oppressions. Diversity provides many opportunities for dumping on other groups: white Christians fear blacks, who distrust Jews, who laugh at gay men, who belittle women, who patronize manual workers, who... The example of relatively homogeneous Norway clarifies how much this dynamic holds us back.

Norway eliminated poverty decades ago, although it was not nearly as rich as the United States in resources and was not a world power able to enforce economic arrangements to its advantage. The powerholders in Norway, as in the United States, resisted policies that would eliminate poverty; as in the United States, the Norwegian rich liked the status quo and argued that poverty is inevitable. Early in this century a social movement grew which united industrial workers with farmers and fishers and idealistic professionals. Together, they were much stronger than the small rich minority and they brought into being a society without poverty. While there were many factors which enabled Norwegians to create their abundant society, the inability of the rich to continue to divide and rule was a major reason why Norway, for example, developed an adequate health care system in the 1940s.[3]

In short, internalized oppression undermines our self-confidence and is reflected in irrational fights inside our groups and inability to maintain strong coalitions with other groups. We need assistance to rebuild our pride and ability to support each other and our allies—a worthy task for every social change group. Building healthy social movements is both a psychological and political necessity.

A Map of the Course

The rich history of social movements means that we do not entirely have to make it up as we go along. We can learn from what worked and what didn't, and the lessons from movements then inform the choices we make as we steer our organizations. The authors have learned a lot about the life cycle of movements from longtime organizer Bill Moyer, who worked with Dr. King on the staff of the Southern Christian Leadership Conference, was a major strategist for the anti–nuclear power movement, and assisted a variety of other movements and organizations. From his study and experience Bill has created a model of how successful movements achieve their goals, the Movement Action Plan (MAP).

MAP is a developmental model; that is, it shows how movements evolve, step by step. Just as we think about human beings with a developmental model (infancy, adolescence, middle age), so also it helps us think about our social change work to have a framework of stages.

Of course MAP is only one way of looking at social movements. We have found it useful, especially in understanding how to steer an organization through the ups and downs of a cause. Bill has kindly allowed us to summarize his model for this book, and we recommend that you read it with the history of your issue in mind.[4] First, a word about models. A model airplane is a simplified version of the real thing. You wouldn't want to fly in it, but it gives you an idea of what it's like and can even be useful for certain tests. An architect often builds a model of a building before the real thing goes up with all its complications. Like all models, MAP is a simplification of a very complex reality, and helps us to face reality with more clarity and perspective.

Bill's model shows us how the developmental stages of a successful movement relate to public opinion, so before we get into the internal life of the movement, we'll take a quick overview of the public. Before there is a social movement around a certain injustice, the body politic seems to be asleep. The toxic waste is being routinely dumped, for example, with office holders looking the other way and public opinion preoccupied with other things. This is stage one.

Then stress builds and the body politic wakes up. In stages two,

17

three and four, more and more of the public notices what's going on, and the office holders get busy reassuring the public that they are taking care of the problem and it's OK to go back to sleep. In each of stages two, three, and four, the movement's growth is in a different place.

By stages five and six the majority of the public agrees with the movement that change is needed (the war should be stopped, or nuclear power is too dangerous, for example). There's a debate, though, about possible alternatives. Stage five is a letdown time for activists, and can be tricky; some movements just die in this stage instead of moving ahead to success.

At last comes success, in stages seven and eight. Many office holders are proclaiming that they really wanted these changes all along, while some of the holdouts are being voted out of office. New groups are spinning off the main reform movement to start the process all over again. Most of the public is glad to stop talking about civil rights, or Vietnam, or nuclear power, and go back to their individual concerns (which, from an activist's point of view, looks like going back to sleep!).

Stage One: Business as Usual

Only a relatively few people care about the issue at this point, and they form small groups to support each other. Their objective: to get people thinking. They do their best to spread the word and often try small action projects.

Stage Two: Failure of Established Channels

A major reason why most of the public does not inform itself and act on an injustice is that people think (or hope) that established structures are taking care of it. "Surely the government is watching out for the safety of our ground water supply." "The government is researching AIDS." "Corporation scientists know which chemicals are dangerous in our workplace and which are not."

In this stage the small groups challenge the established channels. They often do research, or get victims of injustice to file formal complaints. They may sue governmental agencies, or use any opportunities to appeal that exist in the regulations. Usually the activists lose, at this stage, but it is very important that they take these steps. Stage two is essential for change, since large-scale participation will not happen as long as people believe in the established channels.

In fact, you'll find that, by stage two, polls show fifteen to twenty percent of public opinion is leaning toward a change.

In the early 1940s members of the Fellowship of Reconciliation, a religious pacifist group, experimented with sit-ins to integrate restaurants. In Chicago small interracial groups entered lunch counters and demanded service, only to be thrown out or arrested. They were twenty years ahead of their time, but they gained experience and won some new members as a result.[5]

Stage Three: Ripening Conditions/Education and Organizing

Now the pace picks up considerably, because many people who earlier did not want to listen become interested. The movement creates many new groups who work on this issue, largely through education. The groups send speakers to religious groups and union halls; they do marches through their communities; they hold house meetings and news conferences. Much of the content of what they say is refuting powerholders' claims: "People start pollution; people can stop it," "Radiation is not really all that bad for you," "Plenty is already being done to prevent AIDS." This stage can take a very long time or a short time, depending on many things, but constant outreach, through education and forming new groups is essential for the movement to take off. By now, polls show twenty to thirty percent agree that there is a problem or an injustice.

Stage Four: Takeoff

This stage is usually initiated by a trigger event, a dramatic happening that puts a spotlight on the problem, sparking wide public attention and concern. Sometimes the trigger event is created by the movement. In 1963 the Southern Christian Leadership Conference, headed by Dr. Martin Luther King, Jr., focussed on Birmingham,

Alabama, in a direct action campaign which filled the jails and highlighted the evils of segregation with vivid pictures of police dogs and fire hoses. The Birmingham campaign triggered a national and international response, which resulted in the passage of major civil rights legislation.

Sometimes the trigger event just happens, like the near meltdown at the Three Mile Island nuclear reactor in 1979. Three Mile Island (TMI) precipitated massive nonviolent protest and propelled many new people into activity. Previous movement growth had been substantial, but TMI triggered a crisis atmosphere that brought depth and breadth to the movement. MAP shows that the takeoff stage needs the preparation of stages two and three. Nuclear power provides an example we can explore.

Many years before TMI, the Fermi nuclear power plant in the city of Detroit nearly melted down. A disaster similar or worse than TMI threatened then, yet there was no social crisis and no spurt of antinuclear organizing. Why? Because there was no previous social movement challenging the normal channels (stage two) and no education and organizing (stage three). An event becomes a trigger event when a movement has first done its homework.

Because of the high media profile in this stage, many people associate social change with stage four. Often one or more large coalitions form at this time. Celebrities join the movement, the powerholders are shocked by the new opposition and publicity and try to discredit the movement, and polls show forty to sixty percent of the public say they oppose the injustice or current policies. Activists often unrealistically expect a quick victory at this point and work around the clock. Long rambling meetings occur in which new people come and try to make decisions without the necessary procedures in place. The issue is seen in isolation from other issues.

The objectives of stage four are to build and coordinate a new grassroots movement and to win over public opinion. Part of winning the public is connecting the demands of the movement with widely held values (like freedom, fairness, or democracy).

Stage Five: Perception of Failure

There's an old phrase: "Two steps forward, one step back." Stage five is the step back, in the perception of many activists. Numbers are down at demonstrations, the media pay less attention, and the policy changes have not yet been won. The powerholders' official line is, "The movement failed." The media focuses on splits in the movement and especially on activities which offend public sensibilities.

It is the excitement and lack of planning in stage four that create the sense of failure in stage five. By believing that success is at hand, activists can become disillusioned and despairing when they realize they aren't there yet. Hoping to recapture the excitement and confidence of stage four, some groups create Rambo-style actions of anger and violence or become a permanent counterculture sect that is isolated and ineffective.

Fortunately, a great many activists do not become discouraged, or if they do, accept it as part of the process. They treat it like rafters on a river who most of all love the excitement of the white water, but also accept the slow times in between.

Smart strategists lay out strategic, achievable and measurable objectives, and smart movements celebrate them as they achieve them along the way. The powerholders may try to crush the movement through repression at this point, even if they have felt constrained before by a civil liberties tradition. Even repression, however, can sometimes be responded to in the spirit of celebration, as a symptom of achievement.

The FBI was furious. In 1971 someone broke into their Philadelphia area office and stole the files in which they kept information on movement groups. The files were then copied and sent to the movement groups in question, which revealed who the informers were, etc. This was during the Vietnam war, and FBI interference in the anti-war movement was intense.

In order to catch whoever had done it, the FBI targeted a Philadelphia neighborhood where many activists lived. Suddenly strangers with two-day growths of beard, clad in jeans, were lounging around on the street corners. The agents raided some activists' homes in the middle of the night. The activists decided to take the surveillance in a lighthearted way. They came out of their apartments and walked around the strangers, peering at them through obvious holes cut in newspapers. They invited them in for coffee. They handed out leaflets calmly explaining techniques of surveillance.

> *They held a street fair lampooning the FBI, as a fundraiser for the movement. The fair included food and dancing and satirical booths, and the agents were invited. One game featured someone masked and dressed as then–FBI Director J. Edgar Hoover sitting on a plank above a tub of water; for a quarter people could throw a ball triggering a mechanism which dunked "Director Hoover."*
>
> *The FBI retreated before long. The neighborhood activists were having much too good a time at their expense. Adding injury to insult, draft resisters who lived in the neighborhood sued the FBI for violation of constitutional rights and got a cash settlement![6]*
>
> —a Philadelphia peace activist who lived in the neighborhood at that time

Stage Six: Winning Over the Majority

In this stage the movement transforms. Protest in crisis gives way to long-term struggle with powerholders. The goal is to win majority opinion. Many new groups, which include people who previously were not active, are formed. The new groups do grassroots education and action. The issue shows up in electoral campaigns, and some candidates get elected on this platform. Broader coalitions become possible, and mainstream institutions expand their own programs to include the issue.

Until stage six, much of the movement's energy was focussed on opposition (to toxic waste, to war, to homelessness, etc.). In stage six, sixty to seventy-five percent of the public agrees on a need for change. There is now a vast audience ready to think about alternatives to existing policies, and the smart movement offers some. Mainstream institutions can be helpful at this point. One example comes from the anti–Vietnam War movement: universities responded to stage four with peace studies courses and departments, and during stage six many of the scholars involved began thinking about alternatives to the war system.

The powerholders are not passive. They try to discredit and disrupt the movement, insist there is no positive alternative, promote bogus reforms, and sometimes create crisis events to scare the public. The powerholders themselves also become more split in this period.

The dangers of this stage are: national organizations and staff may dominate the movement and reduce grassroots energy; reformers may compromise too much or try to deliver the movement into the hands of politicians; a belief may spread that the movement is failing because it has not yet succeeded.

Stage Seven: Achieving Alternatives

Stages seven and eight could be called managing success. They are tricky, however, because the game isn't over until it's over. In stage seven, the goals are to recognize the movement's success (not as easy as it sounds!), to empower activists and their organizations to act effectively, to achieve a major objective or demand, and to achieve that demand within the framework of a paradigm shift—a new model or way of thinking about the issue.

Goals or demands need to be consistent with a different way of looking at things: a new framework or paradigm. If a civil rights movement simply demands some changes of personnel in government, industry, or schools, it will get more women, people of color or lesbians and gays occupying functions that continue business as usual, including policies which oppress women, people of color, and gays. Social movements are usually much more creative than that, and project new visions of how things can be. A successful social movement, therefore, can gain objectives that, although grudgingly yielded by the powerholders, introduce a new way of operating and of being.

Stage seven is a long process, not an event. The struggle shifts in this stage from opposing present policies to creating dialogue about which alternatives to adopt. The movement will have differences within itself about alternatives, and different groups will market different alternatives to the public. The central powerholders will try their last gambits, including study commissions and bogus alternatives, and then be forced to change their policies, have their policies defeated, or lose office.

It's not unusual for another trigger event to come along (the Chernobyl nuclear meltdown) or be created (the 1965 Selma freedom march in the civil rights movement), which gives increased energy to the cause and wins over still more allies.

23

Each movement needs to develop an endgame which makes sense in terms of its own goals and situation. The fight against nuclear power is an example of change in which there was never a showdown in the United States Congress. Instead, the movement created enough obstacles in the U.S. market to result in a de facto moratorium on new plants, partly by showing them to be unacceptably costly.

Stage Eight: Consolidation and Moving On

The movement leaders need to protect and extend the successes achieved. The movement also becomes midwife to other social movements. We saw growing out of the 1960s civil rights movement, the student movement, the anti–Vietnam war movement, the farmworkers union, the women's movement, the American Indian movement, and others.[7] The long-term focus of stage eight is to achieve a paradigm shift, to change the cultural framework.

The paradigm shift the civil rights movement initiated is still a major part of the U.S. agenda thirty-five years later: diversity as a positive value. In the 1950s, difference was shunned and feared. The rule was to conform. Even rock and roll was attacked as "a communist plot," because it was different from prevailing pop music. Ethnic minorities were taught to be as white and middle class as possible to fit in—that was their only hope (and not a large one) for acceptance. The momentum of the civil rights movement and the movements it midwived continues today as an often intense struggle to see difference differently and to create the structures and processes that make diversity a strength in building community.

While the movement is consolidating its gains and dealing with backlash from those who never were persuaded, the powerholders are adapting to new policies and conditions and often claiming the movement's success as their own. At the same time, they may fail to carry out agreements, fail to pass sufficient new legislation, or weaken the impact of new structures by appointing people who are resistant to the change. A major pitfall awaiting activists in stage eight, therefore, is neglecting to make sure of institutional follow-through.

In this stage, the movement not only can celebrate the specific changes it has gained, but also can notice and celebrate the larger ripple effect it has in other aspects of society and even in other societies. The U.S. movement against nuclear power was inspired by the mass occupations of construction sites by German environmentalists. On this shrinking planet, we get to learn from and inspire each other internationally.[8]

If You Think You're Lost, Check the Map

The course of the river is winding, and sometimes it divides and goes in unexpected directions. Maybe you feel lost; maybe someone wants you to feel lost. Notice that powerholders generally continue the policy you are campaigning against, even while they secretly are laying plans to announce new policies and to prepare the public to accept them. They deliberately hide their defeat from the public, understandably. When you give in to discouragement, you are accepting their definition of the situation. You don't need to—a strategic framework enables you to define the situation.

The last four years of the anti–Vietnam War movement provide our example. The U.S. government stepped up its bombing of Vietnam, exceeding all the bombing of Europe in World War II, and publicly stated its commitment to continuing the war indefinitely. This visible, aggressive policy depressed most antiwar activists, who thought that their ten years of effort had been wasted.

Activists did not know that the U.S. government was at the same time quietly beginning to give up the war. The United States began peace talks in Paris with the North Vietnamese. It then gave in to two key movement demands: withdrawing U.S. troops from Vietnam and ending the military draft. Movement activists saw these moves as irrelevant ploys that undercut the movement's opposition. In the last years, the anti–Vietnam War movement became totally depressed. Then, suddenly, the war ended. Former government officials have acknowledged that the movement was extremely effective in ending the war. To activists at the time, however, it felt just the opposite![9]

You're likely to find yourself beached on that same shore with those activists unless you have a stable strategic framework to use when your work seems discouraging. Check out the MAP—it may keep you going long enough to win!

Notes

1. See Susan Gowan, George Lakey, Richard Taylor, and Bill Moyer, *Moving toward a New Society* (Philadelphia: New Society Publishers, 1976).
2. See, for example, Patricia Jakubowski and Arthur J. Lange, *The Assertive Option* (Champaign, Ill: Research Press, 1978).
3. "U.S. is the top spender on health: U.S. still measures poorly against other countries" reads the headline in *The Philadelphia Inquirer* October 6, 1994, p. 1. The article describes a new international report by a World Bank economist, published in October in the journal *Health Affairs*. For background on Norway's change process see T.K. Derry, *A History of Modern Norway, 1814–1972* (Oxford: Clarendon Press, 1973), especially chapters 6 and 10. The rich controlled state power to enforce their rule; Norwegians used nonviolent action repeatedly and on a mass scale to break the stranglehold.
4. If the model seems useful to you, you'll want to get Bill Moyer's publications, which spell it out in more detail with more illustrations of how it works. Write Social Movement Empowerment Project, 721 Shrader, San Francisco, CA 94117. The model has been picked up by a number of movements. In Australia, for example, the whole issue of *World Rainforest Report* for September 1994 is devoted to MAP. Bill Moyer is also available to lead workshops which apply the model to your specific issue.
5. Robert Cooney and Helen Michalowski, eds., *The Power of the People* (Philadelphia and Gabriola Island, B.C.: New Society Publishers, 1987), pp.151–52. A contemporary example of a practical manual which shows how small groups of activists can lay the educational groundwork for campaigns is Richard K. Taylor, *Peace and Justice Ministry: A Practical Guide* (New York: Harcourt, Brace, 1994) p. 90.
6. *Philadelphia Resistance v. Mitchell*, 1972; representing the plaintiffs were Kairys and Rudovsky.
7. For more on the U.S. context, see Dick Cluster, ed., *They Should Have Served that Cup of Coffee* (Boston: South End Press, 1979). Canadian social historian Darryl Newbury has called our attention to some key books which describe Canadian experience with social movements. These follow with his annotations:
   Joan Sangster, *Dreams of Equality: Canadian Women on the Left* (McClelland & Stewart, 1989). Very good study of women & social change movements in the mid-twentieth century.
   Bryan Palmer, *Working-Class Experience* (McClelland & Stewart, 1992). A good overview of the history of class and the labour movement.
   John Sewell, *Up Against City Hall* (James Lorimer & Co, 1972). This is a personal account of urban radicalism in the late sixties & early seventies written by a community activist who would later become Toronto's mayor.
   Darryl Newbury, *Stop Spadina: Citizens Against the Expressway* (Commonact, 1989). Short monograph examining the campaign of community activist to stop the building of a major expressway through downtown Toronto.
   Bryan Palmer, *Solidarity:The Rise and Fall of an Opposition in British Columbia*, (New Star, 1987).
8. A dramatic example of the international ripple effect is the 1944 overthrow of the Salvadoran military dictatorship by a student movement. The students in next-door Guatemala were inspired, and in the same year threw out their own military dictatorship. See George Lakey, *Powerful Peacemaking* (Philadelphia and Gabriola Island, B.C.: New Society Publishers, 1987), chapter 3.
9. Bill Moyer, *Movement Action Plan* (San Francisco: Social Movement Empowerment Project, 1986).

Chapter 2

POWER FOR THE JOURNEY

Power and Empowerment in Social Movements

THE RIVER OF THE FREEDOM STRUGGLE IS ABOUT POWER. HOW DO WE respond to the challenges of white-water turbulence or the river ice? How do we empower ourselves and those with us on the journey? How do the several faces of power show up in our organizations? When do we accept the cost of tension in order to move the raft along? The process of exploring and learning about power begins in this chapter, with nine guidelines to consider.

Develop an Analysis of Power

Few elements in an organizational culture are as important for success as its view of power. The authors find Starhawk's analysis a useful starting place; she draws on rich experience as a political activist, therapist, witch, and researcher.[1]

Starhawk distinguishes among three kinds of power: power-over, power-from-within, and power-with. The first kind, power-over, is the operating style of most institutions. A multinational company pulls a factory out of a community in the United States or Canada and moves it to Taiwan or Mexico, exercising power-over the town and its suddenly unemployed workers. A state legislature refuses to allow citizens to smoke marijuana legally because it believes it is for their own good. A white city council reorganizes voting districts to divide the growing Latino vote. A religious denomination run by heterosexuals refuses to allow open homosexuals to work as ministers. These are examples of power-over, the domination of one group by another.

The bad news about power-over is not only the diminishment of those who are oppressed, but also the enormous attachment powerholders have to their position of domination. Such an attachment, in fact, that many of them will lie, cheat, and injure, or pay others to lie, cheat, and injure, to maintain their power-over. This is true despite the fact that they are often personally nice people, and they themselves pay a price of guilt, denial, and alienation for the privileges they have.

Life would be easier if power-over appeared only on the societal level. Unfortunately, domination is a pervasive theme which also shows up on the levels of social movement, organization, and individual. In some social movements eighty percent of the activity is done by women and eighty percent of the leadership spots are taken by men. In organizations, the theme of domination can appear in many ways: an autocratic director, overweening influence by the chief funder, a highhanded board of directors, or bare subsistence wages paid to staff. In social change organizations, the domination frequently may be softened by genuine caring and take the form of paternalism: "We'll look out for you, make your work go better, and be nice to you—as long as we remain in firm control and you suppress your own need to grow and become more assertive."[2] On the individual level, volunteers and staff

> The president of the seminary went off the wall when "his" students occupied the boardroom which he'd recently refurbished. He was a pacifist and the students were scrupulously nonviolent, but in his rage he started to call the police to arrest them even though the local jail was a notoriously violent place. It took the dean and senior faculty to calm him down and get him to agree to negotiate with the students. I'd always found the president a charming man, but that day I saw the other side of his paternalism.
>
> —*faculty member of the liberal theological seminary*

28

play all sorts of games that reflect the cultural theme of power-over, and the more insecure people are in relation to the organization, the more likely the members are to act out their scripts of domination and submission.[3]

Power-from-within is the ability to achieve goals, express ourselves, and to grow. From this power comes an awareness which shows up as humility, patience, compassion, courage, and self-assertion. You've seen it in long meetings when the tension grows, and someone is able to keep paying attention, keep a sense of humor, and keep acknowledging the others in the room. Power-from-within is described movingly by Starhawk as a center of creativity, which can sometimes be accessed most deeply by confronting and moving through our fears.[4] Power-from-within is a positive energy for work and play, struggle and integration, which can enliven our organizations for change.

Power-with is the ability to bond as equals, work as a team, and struggle collectively. This power of solidarity is potentially so great that powerholders put enormous energy into splitting up those they dominate: in industry, for example, there is quite a history of creating distinctions between job classifications that lead workers to see each other as superiors and inferiors, rather than sharing a common lot. Divide-and-rule is an essential strategy of domination precisely because if we human beings are left to our own devices we may over time discover power-with and unite to change our condition!

> We want you to stir up as much bad feeling as you possibly can between the Serbians and the Italians. Spread data among Serbians that the Italians are going back to work. Call up every question you can in reference to racial hatred between these two nationalities; make them realize to the fullest extent that far better results would be accomplished if they will go back to work. Urge them to go back to work or the Italians will get their jobs.
>
> —U.S. Steel corporation's instructions to strikebreakers, 1919[5]

Because we see power-over almost everywhere we look, are we to conclude that domination is human nature? Writer Riane Eisler argues

29

in her book on human evolution that we humans have not always and everywhere organized ourselves through power-over; on the contrary, through most of our evolution our species created "partnership societies" instead. If she is correct, domination is not programmed by our human nature. What we have had these past few thousand years is a recent deviation from the mainstream of evolution. Since domination is learned, we can unlearn it, leaving hope for learning another way of using power. The cause is not as hopeless as we may sometimes feel.[6]

Fortunately, power-over has a major flaw. Structures of domination are not as strong as they appear, although the weakness is a fairly well kept secret. The secret is domination depends on the willingness of the dominated to go along with the program.

Even entrenched military dictatorships have been overthrown when the people rise up and refuse to cooperate. The Filipinos in 1986 threw out dictator Ferdinand Marcos after years of struggle they called "people power." In 1989 the Chinese dictatorship almost fell and Communist regimes in East Germany and Czechoslovakia did collapse from widespread noncooperation.[7] These are dramatic examples of the same power which can be tapped more fully through direct action in North America.

Power-over can be challenged when those who are depended upon to cooperate refuse to do so. One reason people do not challenge domination more often is fear of consequences. Fortunately, an art which we are learning more about is how to handle fear. As Starhawk writes, "Where there's fear, there's power."[8] Social movements are expressions of courage; oppressed people draw on power-from-within and power-with to take charge of their future. How consistently this is done depends on how well we build and maintain our organizations.

The Oppressed Become More Powerful in the Leadership of the Movement

Most social movements include both members of the oppressed group and concerned advocates and allies. Look for a power struggle between these two kinds of activists. Who will lead the movement? Who will determine its priorities, its strategic considerations and direction, its tactics? Who will organize and control its resources?

Leaders who come from the more oppressed groups bring increased impact and urgency to movements. The anti–Vietnam War movement, for example, increased its energy and militancy when draft-age youths took leadership. In 1963, largely conventional tactics were used by peace organizations, even in the face of Vietnamese monks burning themselves in protest. When Students for a Democratic Society called the first mass rally in Washington in 1966, the movement shifted into a higher gear both in analysis and tactics. Victims of oppression may initiate action or join movements because they are hurting too much to stand for more abuse, and because they catch a glimpse of a way to act.

Some movements begun by the poor, though resourceful in some respects, lack needed technical and financial resources. Allies and advocates who may have greater access to resources and information needed by the poor can play a valuable role in the movement. They may join because of their values, ideological frameworks, empathy, or recognition of need. Important as they are, they are not necessarily the cutting edge or central force of the movement. Those engaged in economic struggles, who are not themselves directly injured must face important issues. Do they sometimes reduce their militancy and counsel moderation because they are more comfortable than those who are suffering directly? If they have had more schooling than the victims, do they assume that gives them a greater capacity for leadership? A low-income leader in the struggle for housing shares this perspective:

> Don't tell me that a low income mother who has witnessed her three children burned up in a house fire caused by a faulty kerosene heater used because her gas was shut off is unfit to lead this struggle. She has a personal vendetta....She'll fight harder than anybody who's out here just reading books and talking a bunch of bullcrap because it sounds good and feels good. She will fight because she has a personal stake, because they hurt her. Those are the kinds of fighters we need and I'll follow her anywhere, anytime.

Some movements are started by middle class idealists who are not immediately impacted by the problem or who, for one reason or another, have some insulation from the worst of it. Environmental

31

organizations sometimes start this way, or human rights organizations like chapters of Amnesty International, groups in solidarity with Third World liberation movements, or antihunger groups. The National Organization for Women was started by victims of oppression—women—but the initial agenda did not include the issues of poor women, women of color, or lesbians, who are most in need of representation. Over time, tension emerges over who is left out of leadership, and that tension is a growth point for the organization. By facing the challenge of inclusion and acknowledging leadership from those who are most directly impacted, groups can become more powerful and more effective.

> We, the victims of poverty, must go back to basics; hit the streets and organize by the thousands. We are over sixty million strong. We have the necessary knowledge of our needs: food, clothing, shelter.... We will not sit by and wait for a leader because we are all leaders.
>
> —*welfare recipient in an East Coast city*

Focus Your Organizing on Resources, Not Scarcity

There's nothing more empowering than knowing we have choices. One choice activists have is how we interpret a situation that needs change.We become fearful and angry when we describe the proverbial glass as half empty instead of half full. Anyone will despair if they stare long enough at a half-empty glass. If, on the other hand, we see the glass as half full and we consider ourselves deserving an entirely full glass, we are more likely to act in a consistent and sound way. A political activist and father tells this story:

One morning I got very upset with my family, realizing that it needed a lot of changing to be the home where I could relax and go back to my organizing job refreshed, and at the same time feeling inadequate and down on myself as a father. Nobody was around to talk with at the time. Finally I got out my journal and wrote at the top of a fresh page, "What I have going for me as a father." At first I could hardly think of anything, but once I started, the list grew, and as the list grew, I started to feel better and added more to the list. By the time I was finished I had a completely different, "can do" attitude, and began to strategize on how to make my family the home base I deserve.

As in this anecdote, seeing the cup half full may mean noticing what qualities we and our organizations have going for us. Or it may be noticing what resources in the outside environment can be mobilized for change. Either way, the method is resource-based organizing.

Focusing on resources instead of scarcity is easier said than done. Sometimes, we need to let go and feel our despair before we can see the resources. The suppressed anger, fear, and disappointment which most activists carry around can block us from perceiving resources that are right in front of our face. Our most revolutionary first step may be to allow ourselves to feel the feelings and release them. Choose your time and place to do this—it doesn't make sense to spread despair in the organization and sink the morale of others. A good time and place is with a friend who has strong listening skills. Joanna Macy has done pioneering work in assisting activists to come to terms with despair. Originally developed in the context of the threat of nuclear war, workshops designed by her and her colleagues are now used by enviornmentalists and others.[9] A peer counseling process which is used by many activists in a variety of movements is Re-evaluation Counseling (also called co-counseling).[10]

Resource-based organizing values diversity. Ignoring women in the organization, making people of color invisible, keeping gays in the closet, and discounting the opinions of elders and youth reduce the resources available to a movement. Similarly, writing off a community member as "redneck," "yuppie," or "fundamentalist" is a way of rejecting feedback and reducing the resources available to a movement.

Resource-based organizing values time and patience. Italian grassroots organizer Danilo Dolci moved to Palermo, Sicily, knowing that community organizing there meant eventually going head-to-head with the Mafia. He spent a dozen years identifying and building resourcefulness among the people before launching campaigns and winning victories, and he handled the confrontation with the Mafia without getting killed. Activists often have trouble with being that patient if our culture emphasizes "now" rather than history. Two approaches that assist us with our impatience are to read the history of social movements and to develop strategies based on developmental stages of social change.

Don't Forget That Problems Are the Raw Material of Empowerment

When we are under pressure we want the organizational problems we face to go away. That's the "half-empty" way of looking at our world, precipitated by the depleted feeling we have when we experience too much stress. We can decide to see the organizational problems facing us in a "half-full" way, as an opportunity for growth. Solving them builds our problem-solving muscle, and the resulting growth of the organization often brings new and more challenging problems to our agenda.

Social change leadership is a process of problem solving through which we gain the chance to tackle bigger problems (and also gain greater satisfaction through larger impact). The Polish workers movement Solidarity gives a recent example of this process. It began with a reconciliation between radical intellectuals and discontented workers: that was the first problem solved. As it grew, it learned to solve other problems, such as how to manage a large strike and occupation without allowing violence that would divide the movement. When it became widespread and deeply rooted enough to threaten Communist Party control, it had to solve problems of communication, action, and leadership under martial law. Because it proved itself under those conditions of repression—a very challenging organizational task—it "earned" the chance to run the whole country. Solidarity took over the government from the communists, who had discredited themselves partly by their inability to solve the problems facing Poland. While solving the earlier problems is certainly no guarantee that a movement can solve later problems (like creating a new Polish economy which works for everyone), solving the earlier problems is necessary even to have the opportunity.[11]

Problem solving, in short, is empowerment in action.

34

Complaining about problems, on the other hand, dramatizes powerlessness. A group that is ready to let go of complaining will find that this book's problem-solving techniques increase the pace of empowerment.

Provide Services in a Movement-Building Context

First, be clear about whether your group wants to provide services to people or to organize them. In their manual, *Organizing for Social Change* Kim Bobo, Jackie Kendall, and Steve Max illustrate the difference:

> A housing organization was unclear about the difference between providing services to tenants and organizing them. The staff thus did a little of both, considering them to be the same thing.
>
> A man from a building to which an organizer had been assigned, came into the office. After being interviewed about his problem, he was advised to go to Legal Assistance and get a lawyer. The man said, "That's too much hassle," and he left. The organizer remarked, "See, that's why we can't ever get anything going in the building, nobody cares enough to do anything." The organizer didn't make the distinction between an individual problem requiring a lawyer, and a building-wide issue that could be addressed by organizing. More to the point, the organization as a whole made no such distinction because, in its underlying model, its function was neither clearly service nor clearly organizing. As long as it was "housing," they did it.
>
> Had there been a clear organizing model, the staff member would not have made a referral. Instead, she would have gone back to the building with the man, talked to the other tenants, and seen who had the same problem. Even if the problem was an individual matter such as non-payment of rent, if many other people were also behind, the tenants might have tried to negotiate a payment plan in exchange for improved conditions. If legal action to improve building services was required, the action should have been brought by all the tenants, not one individual. If all else failed, then helping the man to get a lawyer would have been appropriate.
>
> On the other hand, if the organization had a clear service model, not an organizing model, then the staff should have phoned Legal

Assistance at once, explained the man's case, had the man talk about the case over the phone, and made an appointment for him. Perhaps someone would even have driven him there.

Unfortunately, because the staff was unclear about what was being built, the man's request for help was handled inappropriately. The result was neither service nor organizing.[12]

Second, make your choice about the mission in the context of the larger process of social movements. There is a history of grassroots groups agitating to change bad conditions, then getting grants to provide services to those hurt by the bad conditions. In the process, the group often loses its ability to fight for change in the structures that create the mistreatment in the first place. While some activists will righteously attack this process as selling out, the usual situation is not so dramatic. Compassion for immediate suffering, the stress of setting up a new organization without sufficient experience or skill, a sense of obligation not to let the agency collapse in a heroic, principled stand, and the pressures of professionalization all contribute to the change in mission.

To solve this problem, the action group can create an agency separate from itself to do direct service. While some of its members may shift to the agency, many members can stay with the group and claim its offspring agency as a victory, using it as part of their track record of success. In setting up the agency, the group can experiment with alternative structures. For example, bylaws can require the board, or board and staff, to be composed largely of clients, in order to institutionalize self-help. The agency then can be an empowerment tool that contributes to building the movement. A program that builds democratic leadership skills, diversity consciousness, organizational skills, and awareness of movement history can further build the movement. The agency can also be part of the base of operations of the movement, because of its resources and personnel. While not ordinarily engaging in direct confrontation (unlike its mother group), it can be an informal ally in the larger effort.

Accept the Reality of the Powerholder's Strategy of Cooptation

One of the ways that fear does not serve us is in our fear of cooptation. The reality is that some portion of any oppressed group will be offered rewards by the system and will choose to give up militant struggle. The typical way that cooptation happens with an identity group like people of color, Jews, or women is that social class becomes the dividing line: after struggle by the group as a whole, some members of the oppressed group are allowed into upper-income jobs and these people change their point of view.

The "half-empty" way of looking at this dynamic is to list the social movements which have been partly coopted—some of the labor movement, the women's movement, and the civil rights movement, for example. The "half-full" way of looking at this dynamic is seeing that even the more conservative wings of these movements remain more progressive than the average citizen, and continue to push for policies that are generally an improvement over the status quo, and that, time and again, people and groups which seem to have been coopted are potential allies in the next campaign.

Once we accept the reality of this dynamic, reduce our fear, and give up the cry of "betrayal," we can roll up our sleeves and take some cooptation-reduction measures. These include: projecting a vision of a transformed society that is qualitatively superior to the alienation of those who choose "a separate peace;" creating a movement that honors the personal work of reducing internalized oppression, that takes seriously power-from-within, and building a spirit of solidarity among movements and organizations, which challenges the individualistic, competitive ethic that supports the pattern of "getting mine."

Ask the Question: "Who Will Pay?"

The answer to the question of who pays is informed by the existing structure of domination. If an organization ignores the question, the powerholders will make concessions to one group by penalizing another.

In the 1990s, U.S. activists are still paying for this mistake, made in the 1960s. The civil rights movement challenged the federal

37

government to deliver justice for African Americans. The choice made by the Democratic Party on how to respond to the civil rights movement was fateful for its own future and revealing for us today.[13] Democratic leadership in the Kennedy-Johnson era was besieged by the numbers, the militancy, and the moral high ground taken by the civil rights movement; the result was a fracture in the Franklin Roosevelt coalition of the Old South, urban, working-class ethnics of the North, and liberals. The Republicans exploited this crack, widening it in each campaign with coded appeals to the racism of white working people, predicting that their taxes would be raised to spend on black people. White working people had not until then minded voting for "tax-and-spend" Democrats, since Democrats spent the money on programs that white working people wanted, like social security and education. When the Republicans pointed out, largely in code, that their taxes would be diverted to programs specifically for blacks, baby "Reagancrats" were born.

The Republicans were not making this up. Dr. King was calling for a "GI Bill" for blacks; others were calling for reparations; Lyndon Johnson declared a "war on poverty" which was seen by all as a war on black poverty. And the money to pay for it did, in fact, come from increased taxes on the working class. White taxpayers watched civil rights groups leaning on the president, the president giving in, and their taxes going up.

This story is interesting because the Democratic leadership did have other options for getting the money to pay for economic and racial justice. They could have cut the military budget, a very large pool of waste and irrelevance. They could have raised taxes on the rich, who could easily afford it. For real change, they could have done both. Their choice to raise the money from working people reflected who actually owned the Democratic Party even in that period when progressive Democrats and labor had a larger voice than today.

The choice the Democrats made is significant, with a valuable lesson for environmentalists, advocates of children, housing activists, and every cause whose success is going to cost substantial money. Success requires that you address tax equity and militarism. If you ignore these, all you can hope for is more attractive rhetoric from the White House and some reshuffling of the burden from one group to another, with resultant divisiveness.

Make More Use of the Power of Direct Action

Groups and coalitions often avoid the question "Who will pay?" because they assume they don't have the power to follow through on alternative answers. It can seem more realistic simply to demand a response from the powerholders than to make a further demand like "Take the money from the military!" Sometimes it is realistic. Sometimes, however, groups ignore the additional power of direct action.

A health care coalition including labor, seniors, religious groups, consumer groups, and others worked for years to push for universal health insurance. The strategy of the core leadership was to start out demanding less than they wanted, to broaden their coalition and reduce the opposition; they confined themselves to petitions, letters, lobbying, etc. In the process, they lost the participation of a number of groups who felt the passion of urgency and also had experience with direct action; for them, the coalition was too tame.

At the eleventh hour, when the cause was clearly lost, the leadership turned in desperation to the possibility of direct action. They no longer had links to a sizable number of people who could apply "street heat," and were left with nothing meaningful to do.

Here again, strategy needed to be influenced by a power analysis. Knowing that insurance companies and other conservative interests had already poured millions into the coffers of the Congress meant that "people power" needed to be mobilized to have any hope of success.

Millions of activists have confronted powerholders in this century by using nonviolent direct action: neighborhood organizations, peace and student groups, civil rights groups, lesbian, gay and bi activists, environmentalists—too many to list.[14] ACTUP, a relatively small network of groups working on the AIDS issue, surprised many by moving and shaking the health establishment through their militant direct action tactics.[15] In the 1990s there is a trend among labor unions to borrow a page from the civil rights movement and do all-out nonviolent campaigning with civil disobedience instead of relying on their traditional strike.[16]

Like white-water rafting, direct action has all the excitement an organizer needs for a sagging campaign; used correctly, it builds stronger movements and more empowered individuals.

What has been learned so far about using nonviolent action to confront power? Some of the lessons are what nonviolent action is not.

Nonviolent action is not a substitute for the hard work of organizing. The late president of the United Farmworkers, Cesar Chavez, led repeated nonviolent campaigns. He said, "The biggest mistake made by individuals and groups seeking change is the failure to choose tactics carefully....Too many times they expect quick change with little effort."[17]

Nonviolent action is not something used only by people with a philosophical commitment to pacifism. In fact, it is mostly used by nonpacifists, for the sheer pragmatic value of it![18]

Nonviolent action is not a guarantee of security for activists. When a movement threatens power, profit, and property, the powerholders usually try to protect their position with violence. But this much is clearer now: the powerholders are less able to use violence against nonviolent movements than against violent movements.

Nonviolent action is no longer as surprising an approach, and more powerholders are now aware of (and prepared for) its use. In the late 1960s, for example, the Philadelphia police unit charged with handling demonstrations had as required reading the movement handbook by Martin Oppenheimer and George Lakey, *A Manual for Direct Action*. This forces activists to become more creative and more strategically sophisticated.

Nonviolent action is no substitute for doing strong media work. Nonviolent tactics sometimes get good media coverage and sometimes not; ongoing media outreach is necessary to support your cause.

Nonviolent action is not a set of tactics that can win without a smart strategy. Campaigns can be lost even with heroic use of imaginative tactics, if the strategy doesn't make sense.[19]

What is nonviolent struggle, then? How can organizers look at it in a new way? Nonviolent action is a technique of struggle that has three very different uses for organizers.

The most common use is for social change campaigning.[20] Almost every day a large newspaper will include several reports of nonviolent action. Chosen at random, the September 21, 1994, edition of the *Philadelphia Inquirer* included:

- Front page: "Shooting victims' shoes make silent statement at Capitol"—a gun control demonstration in Washington, D.C.;
- Page 3: The Nobel Peace Prize–winning leader of the Burmese prodemocracy movement under house arrest;
- Page 21: Haitian demonstrators beaten and killed by the police;
- Front page of business section: U.S. and Canadian autoworkers plan to strike.

A very different use of nonviolent action is to defend the status quo. Environmentalist organizers are often finding it a powerful way to frame their organizing, as are inner city organizers who mobilize neighborhoods to fight the drug traffic. As the director of a major environmental organization in the southeastern United States puts it:

We learned by accident that our fights against dumping toxic waste were much easier to organize if we asked people to defend their community. In the beginning, since we were veteran social justice activists, we began to mobilize people who were more on the periphery of a town and work toward the center. Then we found, to our surprise, that lots of mainstream leader types were into it, because they didn't think the issue was about social change, they thought it was defending the integrity of their community. So they had to be into it, you see, because they were leaders. So we organizers finally got it, that we can frame the issue as defense and cast our net much more broadly.

The last use is in third-party nonviolent intervention. In this application of direct action, the "outsider" can enter a conflict situation to reduce the chance of killing, even if both parties have not agreed to the intervention. This methodology is very different from mediation, because a mediator needs the agreement of both parties in the conflict. Third-party intervention has happened informally and often successfully, over the years, although it's not well known. In 1988 in an urban U.S. neighborhood where an antidrug leader was threatened by assassination, neighbors spontaneously decided to accompany the leader and her family wherever they were going until the threat subsided. In India, Mahatma Gandhi directed his "peace army" to interpose their bodies between Hindus and Muslims who were rioting; the experiments achieved some success. Recently

41

organizations such as Peace Brigades International have been forming to apply third-party intervention internationally.[21]

This is not the place to go into detail about refinements of nonviolent technique, but only to say that it speaks strongly to the issues of power. As the Filipinos said when they overthrew their dictator in 1986, it is "people power," and therefore the technique of nonviolent struggle can tip the scales for social movements.[22] With sufficient strategy and training, it can be used to split the powerholders, win new allies, and give a new sense of power to people who have thought of themselves as victims.

When Frustration Mounts and You Seem to Be Losing, Go Deeper

Sometimes the problems seem so pervasive even the problems have problems! We recommend that you regard your frustration as a valuable symptom and pay attention to it. Frequently, it is a message saying, "The obstacle you're facing needs a new angle, more of the same isn't working." The sense that you are losing probably means, "go deeper."

As an individual activist, "go deeper" means to tackle a personal issue that blocks your power-from-within, or your power-with. Your defensiveness may mean you aren't hearing the feedback you need to correct your approach: "Stop paddling! Hold on! Now, paddle hard!" Your internalized oppression may mean you are intent on judging other leaders instead of seeing them as resources, people with limitations, but nevertheless resources for the cause. Your racism may mean that you are isolating yourself from fellow members and allies instead of uniting with them.

On a movement level, "go deeper" means to connect vividly with your heritage. Most movements have rich heritages to draw from. The Mohawks near Montréal, who confronted provincial authority and Canadian federal troops at Oka in order to protect their ancestral lands from being taken over for a golf course, drew on the tradition of clan mother authority and ancient ceremonies in their struggle. African Americans under stress in the civil rights movement went deeper through prayer and praise.

On an organizational level, "go deeper" means to encourage community to emerge in the organization. By community we mean a social environment in which individuals recognize that they belong together and support each others' growth. A social change community adds to the organizational mission a concern for individuals' well-being and full expression of capabilities. It doesn't mean that every meeting must be a potluck and the members need to be romantically involved. It does mean that, while the organizational agenda propels the group, individual development becomes part of the organizational agenda. A social change community is a place where we experience acceptance and support for our development while we do political work.

Community is a matter of degree, and the degree will differ from one organization to another and even shift over time; a group can make conscious choices about this. The need for community is heightened when a group is frustrated, is losing, and needs to go deeper to find more power-from-within.

Two warnings are in order. First, ours is an individualistic culture. Most of us (although this is affected by class and ethnicity) were brought up to think there must be a tension between the individual and the group. Those of us who are most in a "Lone Ranger" mode may feel threatened and even suffocated by the growth of community. It pays to accept the reality of those feelings, rather than to deny them, and also to ask ourselves whether the feelings are simply part of a cultural bias. It's also possible that we're introverts, with a temperamental need for more solitude.

The second warning is that the path to community is generally through a land called "chaos." Therapist M. Scott Peck describes the process well in his book *The Different Drum*.[23] First there is "pseudocommunity," in which people seek inclusion in the group by conforming to group norms, a kind of honeymoon period. Then there is "chaos," in which people struggle by playing their usual games: controllers try to manage the group, rebels try to stage revolution, victims try to gain pity, therapists and missionaries try to save individuals, etc. Frustration rises as these strategies fail. Some organizations go into this stage not intentionally desiring community as a goal; they back into barely controlled chaos and may experience high drama or chronic low morale while the members valiantly try to recapture the earlier productivity and good spirits of the honeymoon days. The chaos stage ends with a breakthrough into community—a stage of group development in which there is high productivity, high morale, and acceptance of cultural and personal differences.

Life is not static, and neither are groups. Over time, communities may cycle back into chaos, in order to achieve a new breakthrough and reach a deeper level of acceptance of diversity and a higher state of excellence in their work. They may also lapse back into pseudocommunity, or develop a bureaucracy to get the work done. A good deal depends on whether there is leadership that nurtures community and is willing to give the sometimes tough loving that communities need.

Patriarchal conditioning devalues nurturing as a "feminine virtue." Since social change organizations are about wielding power, which patriarchy values as a masculine activity, the theme of nurturing is often attacked by activists as "that touchy-feely stuff." The thinking of Martin Luther King Jr. is relevant here; he was a man who knew how to bring people's action to a level where even the White House had to respond.[24] King argued that power is, at its simplest meaning, the ability to accomplish goals. "Power" has become so loaded because it has become separated from the spirit of love. Hence, we have in the world a good deal of loveless power and also powerless love. What we need, Dr. King said, is loving power, or to put it another way, powerful loving.[25]

> **I was part of the movement for community health centers in the early days. It was brutally hard, but the spirit sustained us. We had hardly any money, but we inspired each other with our grit and our love. Over the years we became successful in one sense—the money came in, our organizations became more orderly, board members learned how to run organizations whether or not they had schooling. But at the same time we lost something, we lost the spirit. When I look back, I feel that we didn't stay in touch with our own heritage, we didn't keep rekindling the fire of our own beginnings.**
>
> —*a long-time health care worker with poor African Americans*

44

Principles That Help You Achieve Balance in Handling Power When Organizing for Social Change

- Develop an analysis of power that you can work with in your group. While acknowledging the heavy impact of power-over (even inside our organizations), study the weakness of domination and specifically cultivate solidarity and inner strength.
- Become more powerful with the oppressed in the leadership of the movement. They bring an urgency and groundedness which are essential to getting the most change possible at a particular time.
- Focus your organizing on resources, not scarcity. Be in charge of your perceptions (the half-full glass), handle your emotions constructively, value diversity to unlock resources, and learn from the past.
- Don't forget that problems are the raw material of empowerment. Problem solving is the way movements grow; when the problems seem overwhelming, increase your problem-solving capacity.
- Provide services in a movement-building context. Direct service can be a Band-Aid that disempowers unless it is organized as a base of operations.
- Accept the reality of the powerholders' strategy of cooptation. Instead of living with anxiety about betrayal, accept cooptive pressures and then reduce their impact through vision, personal work on internalized oppression, and building solidarity.
- Ask the question: "Who will pay?" Ignoring this question allows the powerholders to take resources from another group which is suffering.
- Make more use of the power of direct action. It expresses both power-with and power-from-within, with increasing sophistication.
- When frustration mounts and you seem to be losing, go deeper! On an individual level, that means tackling a personal issue which is blocking your power. On a group level, that means going through the process of developing power-with: community.

Notes

1. Starhawk, *Truth or Dare: Encounters with Power, Authority, and Mystery* (San Francisco: HarperSanFrancisco, 1987), pp. 8–16.
2. For more on the paternalist style in social change organizations, see Bruce Kokopeli and George Lakey, *Leadership for Change* (Philadelphia and Gabriola Island, B.C.: New Society Publishers, n.d.).
3. The view of behavior that emphasizes games and cultural programs is clearly presented by Claude Steiner, *Scripts People Live: Transactional Analysis of Life Scripts* (New York: Grove Press, 1974). See also the works of Eric Berne, the founder of transactional analysis.
4. Starhawk, *Dreaming the Dark: Magic, Sex and Politics* (Boston: Beacon, 1988) chapter 4.
5. Jeremy Brecher, *Strike* (Boston: South End Press, 1980), p. 125.
6. Riane Eisler, *The Chalice and the Blade* (New York: Harper and Row, 1988).
7. Several case studies of dictatorships falling to noncooperation are in George Lakey, *Powerful Peacemaking* (Philadelphia and Gabriola Island, B.C.: New Society Publishers, 1987), chapter 2.
8. Starhawk, *Truth or Dare*, p. 9.
9. Joanna Macy, *Despair and Personal Power in the Nuclear Age* (Philadelphia and Gabriola Island, B.C.: New Society Publishers, 1983).
10. Information is available from 719 Second Avenue N., Seattle, WA 98109.
11. See Michael Dobbs, K.S. Karol, and Dessa Trevisan, *Poland/Solidarity/Walesa* (New York: McGraw-Hill, 1981).
12. Kim Bobo, Jackie Kendall, and Steve Max, *Organizing for Social Change: A Manual for Activists in the 1990s* (Washington: Seven Locks Press, 1991) p. 44.
13. See Thomas Byrne Edsall and Mary D. Edsall, "Race," in *The Atlantic Monthly* (May 1991) pp. 53–86, for a careful account of the major parties and racial politics.
14. The deep roots of nonviolent action in U.S. history are shown in the documentary history edited by Staughton and Alice Lynd, *Nonviolence in America* (Maryknoll, N.Y.: Orbis Books, 1995); their book includes documents as recent as the response to the Persian Gulf war. See also Robert Cooney and Helen Michalowski's documentary and photographic history, *The Power of the People* (Philadelphia and Gabriola Island, B.C.: New Society Publishers, 1987).
15. See Jonathan Kwitny, *Acceptable Risk* (New York: Poseidon, 1992). According to Kiyoshi Kuromiya, Education Director for the Critical Path AIDS Project, David Kessler, the head of the U.S. Food and Drug Administration, has acknowledged that ACTUP and other militants forced the FDA to liberalize some of its policies.
16. While the surprising success of Cesar Chavez in organizing the United Farm Workers was an influence, labor's attention to nonviolent action increased considerably when the United Mineworkers of America won a

major coal strike against the Pittston Coal Company in 1989 by turning it into a nonviolent civil disobedience campaign. One account is by Jim Sessions and Fran Ansley, "Singing Across Dark Spaces: The Union/Community Takeover of the Pittston Coal Company's Moss 3 Coal Preparation Plant," in Stephen Fisher, ed., *Fighting Back in Appalachia: Traditions of Resistance and Change* (Philadelphia: Temple University Press, 1993); another is by Jim Green, "Camp Solidarity: The United Mine Workers, the Pittston Strike and the New 'People's Movement,'" in Jeremy Brecher and Tim Costello, eds., *Building Bridges: The Emerging Grassroots Coalition of Labor and Community* (New York: Monthly Review Press, 1990). By 1994, three major corporations in Decatur, Illinois, were facing a combined civil disobedience campaign by autoworkers, rubber workers, and paperworkers; one of the authors was a consultant for that campaign. The farm workers story is told by Mark Day, *Forty Acres: Cesar Chavez and the Farm Workers* (New York: Praeger, 1971).

17. Cesar Chavez reviewing Lakey, *Powerful Peacemaking*.
18. Martin Luther King Jr., *Stride toward Freedom* (New York: Harper, 1958).
19. See Peter Ackerman and Christopher Kruegler, *Strategic Nonviolent Conflict: The Dynamics of People Power in the Twentieth Century* (Westport, Conn.: Praeger, 1994).
20. Among the manuals that are helpful in planning campaigns are: "Direct Action Organizing" in Bobo, Kendall, and Max, *Organizing for Social Change*; Virginia Coover, Ellen Deacon, Charles Esser, and Christopher Moore, *Resource Manual for a Living Revolution* (Philadelphia and Gabriola Island, B.C.: New Society Publishers, 1977); Ed Hedemann, ed., *War Resisters League Organizer's Manual* (New York: War Resisters League, 1981); "Nonviolent Direct Action: A Manual" in Richard K. Taylor, *Blockade* (Maryknoll, N.Y.: Orbis Books, 1977). For the bigger picture of strategic planning, see Ackerman and Kruegler, *Strategic Nonviolent Conflict* and Lakey, *Powerful Peacemaking*, chapters 5 and 6.
21. Founded in 1982, Peace Brigades International (PBI) has been sending volunteers to Central America, North America, Sri Lanka and elsewhere. For more information contact: PBI 2642 College Avenue, Berkeley, CA 94704.
22. Monina Allarey Mercado, ed., *People Power: An Eyewitness History* (Manila: The James B. Reuter, S.J., Foundation, 1986) is a documentary account with extensive photographs of the Philippine struggle.
23. M. Scott Peck, *The Different Drum: Community Making and Peace* (New York: Touchstone Books, 1988).
24. In his book *Why We Can't Wait* (New York: Signet, 1964), Dr. King tells how the movement in Birmingham, Alabama, forced President Kennedy to act on the civil rights agenda.
25. Martin Luther King Jr., sermon, tape recording in possession of G. Lakey.

Chapter 3

GATHERING THE RAFTING PARTY

The Social Milieu That Translates into Social Movements

MANY ACTIVISTS DON'T UNDERSTAND THAT INDIVIDUALS ARE RARELY attracted to a cause as individuals—they are attracted as members of social circles. Activists sometimes imagine that society, when it comes to social action, looks like this:

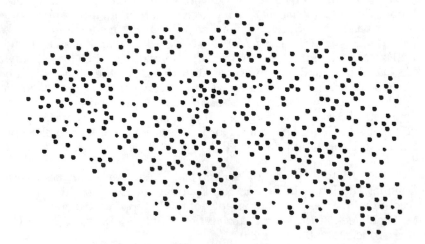

As a result, activists often waste time trying to attract members by leafletting, putting notices in the newspaper, and taping handbills on bulletin boards. Aside from college campuses and other very specialized settings, these anonymous methods are unproductive.

In reality, society looks quite different when it comes to social action:

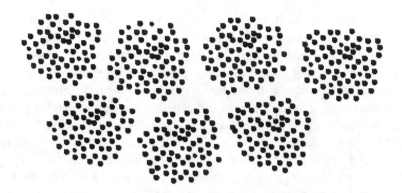

Sociologists call these clusters and informal networks "social circles." They are people connected through an affinity of some kind: religious organization, neighborhood, recreational interest like bowling or softball, etc.

How does a typical activist group get started? In the 1980s many Nuclear Freeze groups started with someone who read the *New Yorker* magazine or listened to National Public Radio. The initiator reached out to others in his or her social circle to form the group. Many groups expanded rapidly, and if the first event (Freeze walk or vigil) was a success, it increased morale and expansion continued. At a certain point in each group's life, the group stopped growing. Often morale problems entered at that point, because the urgency of stopping the arms race seemed greater than ever, yet the group stopped attracting new members.

Group morale sagged because it appeared that "These are all the people in our city who care about the nuclear arms race." Wrong! In many cases the group had exhausted its pool of easily available members, because it exhausted the social circle it was recruiting from. There were still plenty of people in the area who cared about the arms race, but they happened to be in different social circles.

Check out why the people in a social action group you know joined the group. Nine times out of ten, they knew someone already in the group. Social movements, and the groups that compose them, grow through social circles.

Decide the Size Organization You Need and Its Relationship to the Movement

You may be relating to a social movement which is already developed and want to play a specialized role within that movement, such as doing direct action, building a coalition of existing groups, training, organizing in a new sector, conductiong research, etc. Or you might want to get a movement started—a very different task. The mission of your group needs to influence your size and who you want to gather to do the work. For example, maybe you identify with queer liberation and want a group to develop school curriculum materials on homophobia. You decide that a small organization can accomplish that task, and you recruit for it among your own social circle. On the other hand, you might be the first to challenge a plan to dump toxic wastes in your town or reservation. You decide you need a large organization to win on that issue, and you recruit for it from several social circles.

Some activists tackle a goal which requires a large movement, decide to create a large organization to launch that movement, but nevertheless organize only within their own social circle. Unconsciously what they really need is a support group, a group to affirm and validate their point of view or courageous set of actions. They subvert their own political goal because they don't realize how self-limiting it is to work within their own social circle. One possible solution is to create a small team of people who like each other and enjoy working together, and the team then takes on the larger task.[1] Another possible solution is to create a base of political friends who, although not working together on a project, systematically and thoughtfully give each other emotional or spiritual support.[2] If you have a political goal requiring substantial numbers, avoid sabotaging your success through yearning for a cozy and warm group of people like yourself.

For Bigger Potential Growth, Start Your Group with People from Several Social Circles

If what your cause needs is larger numbers, get from the beginning the variety of ages, classes, races, sexual orientations, and lifestyles that provide access to a variety of social circles in your area. Some leaders deliberately put off starting a new organization until they get the combination of people on the ground floor that will allow for the growth they need to accomplish their mission. Being clear about social circles is especially important in coalition work, as this gay activist with long experience working with organized labor describes:

> We have assumed that organizing in the late twentieth century means bringing together lots of different people from different places. I just don't believe that is how social change happens. I think that is how we feel that we are doing good work....But in real life, I think that history is pretty clear that the only time that real change happens is when people are organizing around common self-interest. Too often we try to merge the interests of various groups that are not easily merged into broad-based movements that don't make sense at least in terms of affecting real change....The gay movement [for example] pretends that there is some natural unity between a homeless black gay person and a lawyer who is gay. We are basing the unity on our need to feel inclusive. Activists often act as if they have a worldview that applies everywhere.
>
> One of the things I liked about Harvey Milk (one of the first people to be elected to public office as openly gay) was that he represented all of the white gay movement. That was where his power base was, but the district that he ran in was a district that included pockets of very poor people—poor Asians and poor Mexicans, mainly. He developed an agenda for his political leadership that incorporated the gay community which was a different kind of movement—gays were not oppressed economically. He was able to build a coalition under his leadership where he effectively advocated for the interest of poor people in his community at the same time that he advocated for his own community. But he never pretended that the interests were just the same.

Consider Door Knocking As a Way of Developing a Constituent Base

One way of cracking through the limitation of building your constituency only of the already convinced is through door knocking, which is often used in neighborhood organizing.[3] By going house-to-house knocking on doors and talking about the issue, you can find people who are concerned who might never on their own go to a meeting or a demonstration, introduce the issue to people who aren't aware of it, create rapport so that people can be drawn into a new circle, and reinforce the existing affinity of living in the same neighborhood, so people who aren't moved to action this time may become more open later.

Another way to create a new circle is through house meetings. House meetings can be more effective than those in church basements and union halls, because they are less formal, more involving for the host/hostess, and often easier to get to. Whole neighborhoods and towns have been organized through house-meeting campaigns, and the approach was key to the early success of the United Farmworkers in California.

Peace activists in Los Angeles wanted to go beyond the ranks of the already convinced. The Jobs with Peace leadership chose to learn the house-meeting method of organizing. For neighborhoods where they did not have "leads" (persons already known to be open to activism), the field workers stood in front of supermarkets leafletting to find contacts. By following up on those contacts, they identified people willing to host a house meeting in their living rooms and invite their friends and neighbors. At those house meetings, attenders were asked to join the organization and do door-knocking on their blocks, "neighbor-to-neighbor."

In that way voter education and registration reached far beyond those who identify themselves as activists, new participants were found for the cause, and the organization grew a diverse membership base in both ethnic and economic terms.

Create a Variety of Roles with Different Degrees of Commitment Required

You may have heard someone with many years behind them say "You can have an organization of fifty or five hundred—it's still only a dozen people who do the work." In extreme cases it may be just a few who do the work, or only one!

To minimize this dynamic, create a variety of roles: start committees, task forces, ad hoc committees, and special projects. Be active in suggesting that people move from one spot to another to find the role that best suits them. Alice Paul, the Woman's Party leader who guided the direct action phase of the suffrage movement, was known for her interest in moving women from one place to another in the movement to find the best match between person and task.[4] Don't insist that everyone be equally committed: that creates an in-group and the out-group may not see how they can be useful without forsaking the rest of their lives.

> We had a march to bring the tragedy of crack to the public. We had a banner project with the names of all the people and the babies killed by drugs. The banner was two blocks long, and clergy who had never been together were marching together. We involved people from all the community groups —we had the Central American group acting as marshals.
>
> —East Coast African American woman whose organizing experience spanned poverty groups and peace activists

If a Method Fails, Regard It As Feedback

When your constituency is not growing as rapidly as you want, is in decline, or seems very passive, it can be tempting to blame either yourself or them. Here's another approach: regard it as feedback. What motivates people to participate in your organization? What are the benefits to them? Are the benefits short, long, or middle range? Listening is key here, whether you take a formal survey of your constituency or hang out over coffee or a beer.

There are no medals for continuing to do what isn't working. Try something different. Your newsletter isn't getting read? It lies there unopened with the junk mail? Substitute a large postcard with a bright drawing and a few choice words about your program or an action step. Direct mail fund appeals are getting less return? Try a phonathon to increase the immediacy of your contact with your mailing list.

Be innovative, even at the risk of gimmickry! Organizations don't usually die because of too many gimmicks, but many organizations die while doing the same thing over and over.

Be a "Good News" Organizer

Have you met activists who show they are in the know by pointing out the down side of everything? They cut down even the announcement that the mayor is willing to negotiate, the decision of a moderate group to join your coalition, and the broadcaster's interview of your spokesperson.

While some constituents can be attracted to your organization by the negative attitude of your organizers, you'll lose a lot more potential support than you'll gain. You will also pay a high cost in productivity among your core volunteers, since negativity reduces the ability to think flexibly and creatively. Use every opportunity to share good news, as this director of a coalition of groups fighting for changes in federal budget priorities describes:

> *Our staffers frequently fielded phone calls from people wanting literature or some other service. I taught them to use those opportunities briefly to pass along a new, positive development in our program. Even when the news was minor, it was like telling victory stories— it kept our energy up as well as that of the callers.*

Find the Right Balance for Your Organization between Serving the Constituents and Serving the Cause

It's common for people joining an organization to want things in addition to winning the cause—to find a mate, to find sociability, to relieve guilt, to learn new skills, to get leads for a new job, to be affirmed in an unpopular point of view, etc. One way to look at this is judgementally: people ought to be high-minded and transcend their personal concerns in favor of the organization's mission. Here's another way to look at it: some people don't compartmentalize their lives but instead bring the variety of their concerns right into this space.

Organizations range on a spectrum. At one end, an organization keeps the agenda focused on the cause, sits the members in rows facing front, and lets all the personal issues that people bring remain unrecognized. At the other end of the spectrum, an organization may look like a support group, with attention given to the feelings and concerns of its members, who, symbolically enough, sit in a circle.

Make a decision about where the balance is for your group, and then shift that point in the light of feedback. Some of the factors in your decision might be cultural background, life expectancy of the organization (a short campaign or permanent fellowship), and the needs and preferences of the core group which started the organization. Even if your decision is to be very task oriented, the organization will work more smoothly if some of your members look out for the welfare and nurturance of the others in the group. If your organization makes this nurturing role explicit, you are also less likely to "leave it to the women" and act on the sterotype that most nurturing is women's work.

> How to sustain an organization? You do it by giving people meaningful work, being purposeful, celebrating together, acknowledging good work, and creating a sense of community. If you provide these things people will come and they will stay.

Notes

1. For more on this approach see George Lakey, *Powerful Peacemaking* (Philadelphia and Gabriola Island, B.C.: New Society Publishers, 1987) chapter 4.
2. A wealth of practical ideas drawn from experience is in Katrina Shields, *In the Tiger's Mouth: An Empowerment Guide for Social Action* (Philadelphia and Gabriola Island, B.C.: New Society Publishers, 1994).
3. For resources on neighborhood organizing see Kim Bobo, Jackie Kendall, and Steve Max, *Organizing for Social Change* (Washington: Seven Locks Press, 1991); Si Kahn, *Organizing: A Guide for Grassroots Leaders* (New York: McGraw-Hill, 1981); Bill Lee, *Pragmatics of Community Organization* (Mississauga, Ont.: Commonact Press, 1986); Ed Hedemann, ed., *War Resisters League Organizer's Manual* (New York: War Resisters League,

1981); Katrina Shields, *In the Tiger's Mouth: An Empowerment Guide for Social Action* (Philadelphia and Gabriola Island, BC: New Society Publishers, 1994), Lee Staples, *Roots to Power: A Manual for Grassroots Organizing* (New York: Praeger, 1984). On door-knocking specifically, see Katrina Shields, pp. 49–53, and chapter 10 in Bobo, Kendall and Max.

4. A clear account of the suffrage campaign is in Eleanor Flexner, *Century of Struggle: The Woman's Rights Movement in the United States* (Cambridge, Mass.: Harvard University Press, 1959).

PART II

FORTIFYING THE RAFT

Most groups start informally and soon find that in order to launch a more powerful organization many major decisions need to be made. In Part II we address basic structural issues that not only are made by new organizations, but also sometimes need to be remade by existing organizations, given how times and opportunities keep changing.

Both growth and stability bring their own challenges. Since facing those challenges requires choosing and inventing structures, we offer a variety of options to stimulate your group's discussions. Questions of leadership are raised in two chapters: what kind of leadership structure do you want, and how can you deal with issues of authority and control? Once structure and leadership issues are clarified, the organization can incorporate strategic planning into its work—it can map the journey.

Chapter 4

FINDING A BIG ENOUGH RAFT

The Dilemma of Growth in the Group

The "Golden Age"

MOST ACTIVIST ORGANIZATIONS BEGIN SMALL. A FEW PEOPLE MOBILIZE around a crisis, an unmet need, or a moral outrage. The structure is simple; goals, roles, and authority are easily understood. Relationships are key, and most of the people involved are already friends or acquaintances. Some of the energy of the new organization comes from the joy that friends feel from working on a cause together. New members are often drawn into this informal circle of acquaintances who are caught by the urgency of the situation, trust each other, and are simple and direct. Some groups plan to remain small in order to do their task most effectively: research, video production, and training are functions that may be best organized as small teams rather than larger organizations. This chapter addresses organizations which need to grow to achieve their goals.

We call the first stage a primary system, because the activists' relationships to each other are informal and direct, something like extended families or small schools or businesses. The group has an important task and is not simply for socializing, yet it has some of the camaraderie which comes with affinity. Since this is the usual way groups begin, organizations rarely start with cultural diversity. Our society is divided, so social circles reflect that. Overcoming cultural polarization means, therefore, being intentional—either right from the start or later.

In a primary system, group meetings provide the arena for the coordination of tasks and maintenance of morale. The organization doesn't worry about policies and procedures. Instead, it decides most questions in terms of goals based on an unstated set of assumptions. The group may have formed around a leader, but the leadership is generally informal.

Every successful group includes at least one person thinking about the whole group. The person thinking about the whole group may or may not be called a leader. In fact, someone called the leader may be so occupied with strategy, the next demonstration, the media or relating to allies that she or he hardly ever thinks about the group as a whole. Someone thinking about the whole is constantly diagnosing the group. This process may be intuitive, or may include an explicit list. This entire book is, from this standpoint, a diagnostic list.[1] In a primary system, there may be a number of individuals thinking consistently about the whole group, and in that sense sharing leadership. Even in an organization which seems to revolve initially around one leader, the leader may do more coaching, inspiring, and groundwork on the issue than operating in an authoritative manner with the other members of the group.

Most people find this way of working enormously appealing—the simplicity, directness, informality, and social connections—and want it to go on forever. Hence we call it the golden age.

When the new organization becomes known and more people join, a variety of complications and conflicts begin, which fortunately are predictable. What began as a simple and direct response to a problem can suddenly be mired in ill-defined authority, confusion of roles, lack of organization and planning, ineffective hiring, inadequate supervision, and poor communications. Accept the new reality brought by growth and time, and begin to let go of the golden age, replacing it with the secondary system—an alternative structure which can handle complexity and growth.

When organizations become bigger and more complex, they need to operate differently in order to be effective and to be perceived by those working for them as fair, just, and equitable. The informality and ruling by exception which is so frequent in primary organizations does not work as well with large numbers of people. The necessary result is agreement on rules, regulations, standards, and measurable criteria of accountability. Division of labor on a larger scale requires more coordination to keep the whole organization moving toward its goals. More coordination requires clarity about who coordinates what and who makes which decisions.

Why let go of the primary system? One reason is to achieve certain social change goals. A neighborhood group may need to attract sufficient members to be able to intervene powerfully in decisions about zoning and environmental planning. A seniors organization may need to become very large in order to lobby convincingly for policy changes at the state level.

Another reason to let go of the primary system is to include people who want to participate. The amiable disorder in a new, informal organization becomes stressful over time for members who, after dropping things to respond to the crisis, need to catch up with the rest of their lives and still want to participate in the cause. Initially, excitement and urgency can carry us through six hour meetings, but at some point family, career, and personal needs (like rest!) move up the agenda. At that point some members are willing for a steering committee to make more decisions, for division of labor to grow, and for information to be organized formally (through minutes, for example). This is a point in group development when it can lose members beyond normal turnover. If the core group resists the needs of other members, individuals drop out when they realize the only way to stay involved is to sacrifice their other needs. The group also has trouble recruiting new members who aren't willing to make the sacrifice or who aren't looking for a new subculture to join.

> "I don't see many of you here who were with us in the old days," the environmentalist said. "It was great. There were just a few of us in that small suite of offices over the supermarket. We knew everybody, and what everybody was doing, and there was such great spirit, and we all got off on each others' victories. Now we're this big organization and I don't know half the people I see in the halls, much less know what they're doing. It's just not the same."
>
> —*from a staff discussion in a national environmental organization*

A third reason to let go of the primary system is that it often leads to sectarianism. Over time, individuals meet their social needs in the group, deepen their friendships and find their lovers there, and lose some connection with the rest of the world. Individuals lose perspective and become victims of a closed circle of assumptions and beliefs, which over time distances members from how other people see reality.

> At first I thought the socialist group whose meetings I checked out when I was in college wasn't for me because I was working class and they were middle-class professionals. They constantly argued about ideas I didn't know much about, and a lot of the ideas seemed to be more about other countries than this country anyway, and I just didn't have anything to say and when would I ever have time to read all those books they quoted? But now I've looked in on a lot of radical groups and I can see it's not just that they had the middle class obsession with words. A lot of radical groups mainly talk to themselves. Maybe they once in a while talk to a taxi driver, but I'll bet they don't listen. So if they just talk to each other, how would they know what's on the minds of the rest of us?
>
> —an activist in his fifties, reflecting on his political journey

The golden age, in summary, can be prolonged beyond its usefulness. Insisting on the informal primary system can prevent growth that enables accomplishment of some goals. Hanging on to the good old days can prevent the participation of people who want to participate but can't give the hours and spontaneity that are required to "stay in the loop." A primary system can even lead to the group becoming a sect, unable to relate effectively even to its natural allies.

The Secondary System

When you notice growing pains, start to invent your own secondary system. Set up a task force to research various structures; feel free to adapt one that fits your mission and constituency. We have suggested characteristics to assist you in thinking about your situation in terms of organizational operations. By bringing these features to the conscious level, you may start to invent options for your own organization. When you have options, your group can then choose a structure that will meet its needs for a secondary system.

SMALL ACTIVIST ORGANIZATIONS/ PRIMARY SYSTEM SIMPLE	LARGER ORGANIZATIONS/ SECONDARY SYSTEM COMPLEX
Everyone accountable to the whole	Immediate accountability to a coordinator
Friendly, personal	Less personal, permission to be neutral
Emotional openness encouraged	Objectivity encouraged
Informal, few rules	More formal, clear rules and procedures
Appraisals, supervision casual	Appraisals formal, supervision specific
Membership through intention rather than achievement or requirement	Membership through specific criteria (e.g., contribution, service)
Staff and volunteers learn by doing, experimenting	Formal learning and training complements learning by experience
Little formal planning, leadership is reactive	Planning and proactive leadership

Many groups start in a protest or in an urgent desire to meet an overwhelming need, but with little hope that they can accomplish the changes they want. With the growth of the organization comes a possibility of achieving the goal, and a corresponding incentive to strategize and to manage human and financial resources wisely. The organization is ready for skill development in strategizing and managing. A secondary system differentiates among functions, and links them to skills, training, and formal ways of maintaining accountability.

In primary systems people tend to feel connected strongly to each other and the group. In effective secondary systems people tend to know their roles, what's expected, and what success is. Both forms can be highly effective in what they do. Tensions and problems are greatest in organizations caught between the two. What used to work is difficult. Some drop the ball in communicating. Others are not accountable. Relationships are breaking down. Differences in roles and power are becoming apparent yet are not agreed upon, leading to personalization, gossip, confusion, and uncertainty. Anger and frustration increase, yet open conflict may be avoided because of a history of friendship.

Tensions are inevitable if an organization grows or persists over time. It is impossible to keep all of the advantages of the primary system and still grow. Although previous experiences we've had with insensitive bureaucracies may make us determined not to let our movement groups fall into that trap, if an organization wants to grow, the choice is not whether or not to become a secondary system: the choice is what kind of secondary system to become. The next chapter describes a variety of options.

Notes

1. A more convenient list (especially in terms of group functions) is found in Virginia Coover, Charles Esser, Ellen Deacon and Christopher Moore, *Resource Manual for a Living Revolution* (Philadelphia and Gabriola Island, B.C.: New Society Publishers, 1977), pp. 46–47. Once the diagnosis reveals a problem, the person thinking about the whole intervenes.

Chapter 5

SELECTING THE RAFT FOR THE COURSE

Choosing and Inventing Your Organizational Structure

WHETHER YOU ARE STARTING A NEW GROUP, MOVING FROM AN INFORMAL action group to another stage, or having major problems with your already established organization, it makes sense to consider your structural options.

Think creatively to invent the structure that is right for your group. People make assumptions about how an organization should be structured based on their experience with other groups, their lack of experience, what they have heard and read, and their values. A benefit of creating your own structure is that you can flush out each others' assumptions and may thereby avoid some unmet expectations and misunderstandings.

Don't be surprised if not everyone in your group is enthusiastic about this task: everyone doesn't need to be. It's fine that some will prioritize action, or community building, or research. Whether or not each member feels personally drawn to the task of structuring, everyone needs to allow the task to be done. Structure is a key to effectiveness, because it has to do with decision-making and implementation, responsibility and accountability, authority and control. As long as these issues are poorly considered, the group's work and morale will suffer. Those who take on this task need to get feedback frequently from those who are less interested.

Of course your structure influences the people in your group, their relationships with each other, and their feelings about themselves.

Some people work best if they can organize their own work and operate fairly autonomously, while others feel isolated under the same circumstances. Some people find their energy drained and creativity subverted if "the boss" or "management" makes most decisions, while others resent the time and effort spent in participatory decision-making. The goal is to find the right fit between an organization's mission, values, structure, and people.

Activists in a midwestern city are serving people at risk of violence or recently involved in personally violent relationships and situations. They created an organization which combines advocacy and direct service, decentralized collectives and coordination, and has an annual budget of over $300,000. Established to educate the community about personal and institutionalized violence, the organization includes former perpetrators as well as victims of violence. There are nine full-time and twelve part-time staff, and the tasks are performed by collectives within an overall system of accountability. The members of the organization span the ages sixteen to fifty-two and are widely diverse in education and racial/ethnic background.

One of the long-term members of the group describes the organizational structure this way: "Once collective members make peace with the feeling of chaos, the worry that no one of authority is standing over us to ensure that we don't make mistakes or spend all our money, we begin to see some interesting synchronicity and serendipity in the way things get done, fall into place."

Consider the Meaning of Membership

Any ongoing organization sooner or later faces the challenge of its own ability to change. Over the longer term, how does it adapt to changing environment, to changing consciousness, to some doors closing and other doors opening? One answer is to create a structure of broad accountability to the people who care about the cause, for example through a democratic membership base. A democratic membership structure provides a clear way for members to influence the direction of the organization. It can take the form of electing a board at an annual meeting or a mailed ballot, for example. Such a structure provides a check against the core leadership of a group getting out of touch with its constituency.

The specifics of how members can exert their influence need to be spelled out in the organization's ground rules, often called bylaws.* If members exert influence through meetings, state the notification procedures and the minimum number needed at the meeting to conduct business. Most states give formal members of incorporated organizations the right to vote on issues such as election and removal of members of the board of directors, amendment of bylaws, mergers, and dissolution of the organization. State clearly in the ground rules whether decision-making is by consensus or by voting, and if by voting, what percentage of approval is required to make a decision. (Some groups seek the advantages of both consensus and voting by setting a higher standard than simple majority, for example 75 or 80 percent agreement for a vote to carry.)

Membership criteria are important, too. The people who care need to prove it through contributions, so your organization's direction is influenced by people with convictions, not just opinions. People outside the core of the organization, people who are not regular volunteers or committee members, but who may come to the occasional meeting or demonstration, are not immersed in the organizational culture and can have a more objective, impartial perspective to offer. If part or all of the constituency are people with low incomes, the obligations of membership might be defined in other than financial terms, like twice-a-year volunteer work. (Be careful about giving up financial expectation, however—we live in a culture that constantly sends messages that money is the measure of what is important. If we've been brought up here, we are conditioned by those messages to some degree, even if only on a subconscious level. When an organization doesn't expect money from us, it's easy to give less importance to the organization, again if only subconsciously.) The ground rules need to state how members are admitted and terminated.

Whether or not to have formal membership is an important choice. One reason to avoid formal membership is that it is much simpler (no

* The question of incorporating the group is taken up later in this chapter. Whether or not the decision is to incorporate, it is still wise for an organization to have clear agreements or ground rules that clarify how members can exert their influence.

mailings and procedures for annual elections, keeping accurate records about who is entitled to participate, etc.). Geographical dispersal of members may argue against an annual meeting, yet a mailed ballot for election of a board may not work when the board needs to be balanced regarding skills, experience, and perspectives. For some organizations, the most effective solution is to adopt a structure that combines a formal membership category that involves rights and responsibilities with a category of nonvoting supporters.

Many organizations have "memberships" that are not memberships in the sense that members actively participate, for example, by electing a board of directors or voting on policy direction. The confusion can lead to the charge of lack of democracy. If the group wants to be surrounded by a support community that contributes money or volunteer time, why not call those individuals "supporters," "friends," or some other name which fits the organization's mission and style? You may want to undergird the relationship with an exchange, for example, sending a newsletter or discounting admission to events in return for an annual contribution.

A mechanism some groups use to meet the need for feedback and to keep them in touch with changing needs and changing times is an advisory council of thoughtful and strong people who don't mind challenging the assumptions of the core leadership. The advisory council meets with the core leadership from time to time—for example, in an annual retreat. Skillful facilitation is needed to reduce defensiveness on the part of the core leadership and enable the advisory council to be honest and forthright, raising the problems they see as well as the positive achievements. It is helpful to ask the advisory council to respond to specific questions or to provide input on specific issues. If the group is having trouble reaching agreement about membership structure—especially if you notice emotions coming to the surface—you probably need to look at the psychological issue of boundaries and different ways of looking at that issue.[1]

I used to be hard on myself because I was working in groups that didn't have their shit together as far as structure goes. We were always veering off into inefficiency and lack of accountability, or else we got into hyperefficiency and people would do power tripping and it wasn't fun any more. Even at our best times when we were doing really good work, we still didn't live up to my ideals of how a group should be.

Then I read more about the patriarchy and realized that we've been under its grip for thousands of years, and that there is an alternative way of working that has an even longer history but that we lost touch with. And that we've recently been working our way back to partnership but we have this heavy, heavy drag of inherited patterns of domination slowing us down.

So now in working with activists I cut us a break and realize the best we can do is experiment, and find out what works by trying new things that start to reflect our values and still draw on the lessons we and others have learned. I'm much less harsh now, and more interested in imagination instead of judgement.

—veteran East Coast organizer who has worked on the neighborhood, city, and state levels

Invent the Structure that Fits Your Mission, Values, and People

Organizational structures run the gamut from a hierarchy to a collective. In a hierarchy, decisions are passed down through successive levels for implementation. In a collective, decisions are made by the people who will implement them. Most activists value equality and individualism, but often don't know how to use their values to build an organization. There's a lot to consider: the mission to be accomplished, the resources available (both people and finances), the outside environment (including forms of opposition), and the culture or cultures represented by the core activists and the constituency.

More and more organizations these days are structural hybrids. Hierarchies are making use of collective structures such as teams, and organizations that started out as informal collectives are incorporating, establishing boards of directors, and looking more like a flat hierarchy. The environment in which all organizations are operating is changing rapidly. Flexibility and adaptation is necessary for survival. The structure that served well in an earlier stage of a group's life may become counterproductive in a later stage. When an organization is developing a long-range plan for its work, it might consider whether its present structure needs to be clarified or changed in view of new demands or changes in its mission.

> *When I joined the staff of a rape crisis center I found a collective structure which came out of the feminist spirit of equality in the women's movement. There was a board elected by the volunteers, but much uncertainty between board and staff about their responsibilities. The board was very involved in day-to-day operations because, as volunteers, board members were active in all program areas; at the same time, the staff director reported to the board.*
>
> *At the time I came on staff the center got a large government grant, but this only lasted a couple of years which meant that we had to diversify our funding. That decision, in turn, meant that we needed to describe our organizational structure to potential funders.*
>
> *The traditional hierarchical chart was inappropriate to our ideals and to our reality. Instead, we made a chart with a small circle in the center, representing the board, surrounded by a bigger circle representing the staff. From the center there were lines going out, like spokes of a wheel. At the end of the spokes were circles representing the programs, which were operated by volunteers with staff acting as coordinators. The fact that the line went from each program circle to the center showed that volunteers from each program sat on the board. Because each line went through the staff circle, we could see that staff was connected up. It felt great to create a chart that showed our special structure, and it was useful for our members to have a better understanding of how the organization was put together.*
>
> —former director of the agency, which was one of the largest rape crisis centers in North America

Here is an overall perspective to keep in mind when inventing structures: most people do a better job when they get more satisfaction from their work. They get more satisfaction when they see how their own efforts connect with the work of others, when they have input in decision-making, and when they have some control over their work. Both the individual and the organization benefit from clarity about accountability and responsibility.[2]

An organizational chart is a graphic display of an organization's accountability structure. Let us consider some of the possible structures.[3]

Traditional Hierarchy

A pyramid is the traditional shape of a hierarchy. The more levels there are between the top and bottom, the steeper the hierarchy. When there are only two or three levels in the pyramid, it is a flat hierarchy. Decisions are made at the level above where they are implemented. The higher up the pyramid a decision is made, the more impact it presumably will have on the work of the whole organization. People on a lower level may be asked for information needed for decisions made higher up, but they do not participate in making the decisions.

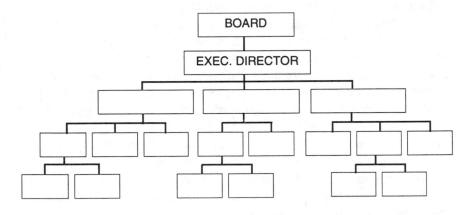

TRADITIONAL HIERARCHY

It appears to be a simple and rational structure. It clearly spells out who is accountable to whom. It does have limitations. Since information has to travel up the pyramid before decisions can be passed down, it slows down an organization's ability to respond to quickly changing demands and opportunities. Also, it rarely fosters individual creativity and cooperation between different parts of the organization.[4]

Teams

One way to combine the needs for participation and accountability is to substitute teams for the usual multilevel management/worker structure. Members of a team depend on each other for accomplishing the team's tasks. Team members may have different skills and levels of experience, but everyone's participation is necessary for the job to be done. They are interdependent. This means there needs to be some overlap of skills and knowledge, so team members can cover for each other in times of emergency. Teams may be true collectives, where everyone participates in making decisions, or they may have a leader who makes certain kinds of decisions and represents the team in relations with the larger organizational structure. Being a team, however, implies participants having input, at least, into decisions at the team level.[5]

Teams can be used at all levels, including with top management. Having a management team accountable to the board instead of an executive director avoids the problems connected with all responsibility resting in one person, and can add both stability and depth to the organization's leadership. One person may serve as team leader, specifically thinking about the functioning of the team as such and not just about organizational decisions that must be made. A management team requires clear expectations about the functioning of the team and the board's responsibilities if serious conflicts arise among members of the management team.

Most organizations need structures that allow them to respond flexibly as conditions change. A metropolitan organization serving children and youth faced declining participation by both children and adult volunteers, and had attracted few people of color. To stem the membership decline and rectify the racial imbalance, it created multifunctional teams. Each team became responsible for programs in a number of geographic areas bridging different racial groups. Individuals continue to do "their job," but now in the context of team planning. Team leaders think about the team as a whole, participate in the work and meet periodically to share ideas and experiences and connect their teams with the wider organization. This formerly traditional organization now has teams below the executive director.

71

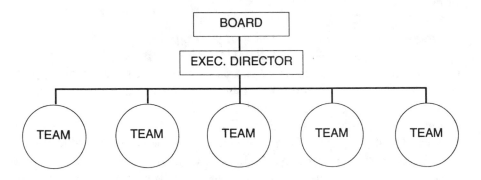

TEAMS BELOW EXECUTIVE DIRECTOR

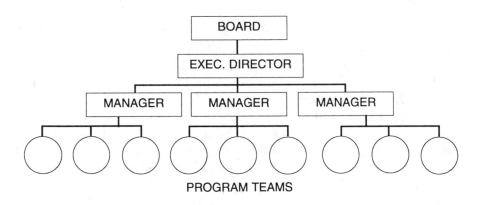

PROGRAM TEAMS

TEAMS BELOW MANAGERS

In another modified hierarchical model the board of directors sets organizational policy, hires the executive director, and assesses how well the mission is being accomplished; the executive operates through a small group of managers, each of whom coordinates the work of a number of teams.

In some models the executive director has been replaced by a management team. Each team member directs, manages, or coordinates an area of the organization's work. There may be a traditional hierarchy below the management team, or the team form may pervade the organization.

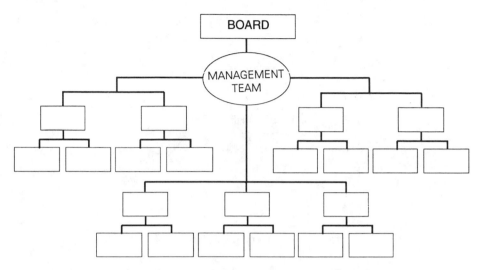

MANAGEMENT TEAM WITH TRADITIONAL HIERARCHY BELOW

MANAGEMENT TEAM WITH TEAMS BELOW

In a flat hierarchy the board may act through an executive director, who implements the organization's programs through an administrative team and a number of self-directed program teams (or in small organizations, individual program staff members).

73

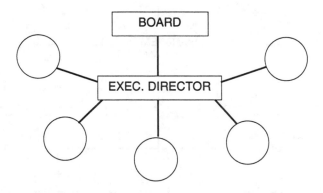

FLAT HIERARCHY

In a council model, representatives from each program team serve on the board of directors. The executive director is charged with administrative functions, including the hiring and firing of staff, and the coordination of the organization's program, which is carried out by self-directed teams.

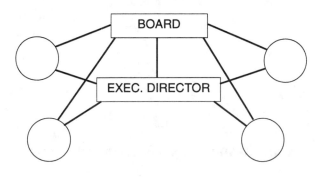

COUNCIL

Nonhierarchical Structures

If the people who make decisions are also responsible for carrying them out, there is no hierarchy. No one is above anyone else. In an organization with more than a handful of members, this does not necessarily mean that everybody is involved in every decision or that skills and experience are the same for everyone.[6]

Many people who were part of the women's movement in the 1960s and 1970s wanted to throw off the dominating shackles of patriarchal structures and, therefore, rejected leadership roles. What they found, as sociologist Jo Freeman pointed out in her landmark article "The Tyranny of Structurelessness," was that both leadership and sustained patterns (structures) developed anyway, as underground phenomena.[7] The informal structure—because it was not acknowledged—was unaccountable, and in that sense highly undemocratic. A democratic collective is one where the members are aware of group process and power dynamics and are willing to work through conflicts together to maintain productivity and accountability.

In a simple collective, each member is a partner to the decisions made by the group and carries equal responsibility with the others for the mission and conduct of the organization. One person may be assigned the role of facilitator, or in Robert Greenleaf's term, the "first among equals."[8] This role may also rotate among the members.

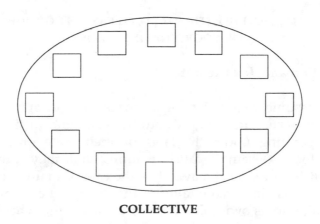

COLLECTIVE

75

A collective can have a coordinating subgroup composed of individual staff members or representatives of teams. This model may be useful for an organization where there are more people involved or where it is useful for external reasons to be able to point to a board or a policymaking and oversight group. Members of the central group are elected by their teams/collectives to make policy for the organization as a whole, to receive grants or other revenues, to approve and monitor the budget, and to ensure that the organization operates in accordance with its own rules and the laws of the land.

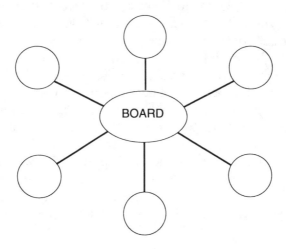

**COLLECTIVE WITH BOARD, OVERSIGHT GROUP,
OR COORDINATING GROUP**

Incorporation and Tax Exemption

Don't assume that becoming a nonprofit corporation needs to restrict your structural options unduly. Sometimes activists assume that incorporating under the laws of their state or province, or applying for tax-exempt status, requires that they adopt a very traditional structure. That may not be the case. Usually the interest of government is in accountablity, including the organization's accountability to its own rules, rather than in saying what those rules should be. We know of very innovative structures which have received tax-exempt, corporate status. The requirement common in Canadian provinces, for example, that the organization have a board of directors and an annual general meeting of the membership may be easy to meet within an innovative context. Here are some advantages and disadvantages of going the nonprofit corporate route.[9]

Advantages:
- Avoiding personal liability: Members of the group will, in most cases, be protected from personal liability resulting from lawsuits that may be brought against the group. (For example: a personal injury suit after someone falls and is injured during an event sponsored by the group.) Exceptions to this protection might be cases in which board members can be shown to have been negligent in performance of their duties.
- Tax exemptions and other benefits: Tax exemption on purchases of equipment and supplies and on federal and state corporate income taxes, reduced bulk mailing costs, nonprofit discounts, access to radio and TV public service announcements, etc., help save money.
- Fundraising: Nonprofit status makes it easier to solicit funds from individuals, businesses, and other organizations in both Canada and the United States. Becoming a nonprofit corporation under state or provincial law is the necessary step before applying to the federal level for tax-exempt status. With that status, you can offer contributors the opportunity to make tax-deductible donations to your organization. Some donors feel able to make larger gifts if they can take credit for them at income tax time. Many foundations will make grants to you only if you have nonprofit, tax-exempt status.
- Employee benefits: People involved in doing the work of the organization can be compensated as employees and be eligible for fringe benefits not available to self-employed persons, such as unemployment insurance.

Disadvantages:
- Incorporation and application for tax-exempt status take time and money, although often less than $200.
- The accountability that comes with a more formal organization

takes time and energy, including such tasks as recording and keeping minutes of meetings, bookkeeping, and filing annual reports with various government agencies.

Watch for program limitations which are imposed by tax exemption, and consider whether they are worth it to you. A nonprofit corporation may engage in any lawful activity which is related to the purposes stated in its articles of incorporation and its bylaws. Getting status as a charitable or educational organization means applying to the federal level in both Canada and the United States. For example, in order to be granted 501(c)(3) status under the U.S. Internal Revenue Code, an organization must

- be organized for charitable, educational, religious, literary, or scientific purposes,
- not participate in polical campaigns for or against persons running for public office,
- substantially limit legislative or grassroots political activities. This means that they cannot urge people to vote for or against particular pieces of legislation or candidates, but they can inform their members and the public about the issues involved.

If the U.S. Internal Revenue Service (IRS) finds that a 501(c)(3) group is organized for goals that can only be attained through legislative action or that its work is focused on the attainment of such goals, rather than on nonpartisan analysis and information dissemination, IRS can deny or revoke its 501(c)(3) status. Writing your group's bylaws and mission statements in ways that do not wave red flags at the IRS is therefore important. Describing the organization as an action group would be such a red flag because, for the IRS, this implies political campaign activity. A sister organization can be established to do the legislative work. This group, classified as a social welfare organization, could even be tax-exempt; it couldn't, though, receive tax-exempt donations like a 501(c)(3) organization can.

In Canada, charitable status is not likely to be given to advocacy organizations even when they steer clear of the legislative process. Again, setting up a sister organization to do advocacy may be the best approach.

Does it make sense for an organization to go the route of nonprofit incorporation and, beyond that, IRS 501(c)(3) status? It really comes back to the mission, values, and people involved. If the group is a grassroots protest group which specializes in civil disobedience and legislative pressure, the incorporation route may be cumbersome, restricting, and its financial advantages of little value.

Experiment with alternative structures and keep the ones that fit your values and mission. In recent decades some activists have been unhappy with the traditional organizational chart of board/staff/volunteers, feeling that it builds into activist organizations the inequality and dominance of the larger society. Recent theoretical support for innovation comes from Riane Eisler's book, *The Chalice and the Blade*, which argues that vertical ranking is characteristic of dominance structures and that the major alternative in human evolution—partnership—develops ways of working which link people in a more horizontal way.[10]

Even if you are working within a very traditionally structured organization you can increase your own flexible space. The physicist Fritjof Capra shows a way as he challenges the metaphor of the pyramid even for traditional organizations. He argues that hierarchy distorts our understanding of the genuine relationships within the organizational system: "The important aspect of the stratified order is not the transfer of control but rather the organization of complexity." We'll understand organizations better, he says, by using the metaphor of a tree. "As a real tree takes its nourishment from both its roots and its leaves, so the power in a systems tree flows in both directions, with neither end dominating the other and all levels interacting in interdependent harmony to support the functioning of the whole."[11]

Notes

1. Starhawk, *Truth or Dare: Encounters with Power, Authority, and Mystery* (San Francisco: HarperSanFrancisco, 1987) chapter 6: "Risking the Boundaries."
2. See Marvin R. Weisbord, *Productive Workplaces: Organizing and Managing for Dignity, Meaning and Community* (San Francisco: Jossey-Bass, 1987), and Peter B. Vaill, *Managing as a Performing Art: New Ideas for a World of Chaotic Change* (San Francisco: Jossey-Bass, 1989).
3. The Canadian organizational development consultant Gareth Morgan describes a variety of options for organizational structure in his book *Imaginization* (Newbury Park, Calif.: Sage, 1993).
4. For more on the limitations of traditional hierarchies, see Robert K. Greenleaf, *Servant Leadership: A Journey into the Nature of Legitimate Power and Greatness* (New York: Paulist Press, 1977) and Peter B. Vaill, *Managing as a Performing Art*.
5. Key references on the use of teams include Peter M. Senge, *The Fifth Discipline: The Art and Practice of the Learning Organization* (New York: Doubleday, 1990); William G. Dyer, *Team Building: Issues and Alternatives* (Reading, Mass.: Addison-Wesley, 1987); Carl E. Larson and Frank M.J. Lafasto, *Teamwork: What Must Go Right/What Can Go Wrong* (Thousand Oaks, Calif.: Sage Publications, 1989). Weisbord, *Productive Workplaces*, is also useful.
6. For examples of nonhierarchical organizational structures, see Starhawk, *Truth or Dare*, pp. 152–158.
7. Jo Freeman, *The Politics of Women* (New York: David McKay, 1975).
8. Greenleaf, *Servant Leadership*.
9. Lawyer Anthony Mancuso has written an excellent book for nonlawyers on *How to Form a Nonprofit Corporation* (Berkeley: Nolo Press, 1992).
10. Riane Eisler, *The Chalice and the Blade* (New York: Harper and Row, 1988).
11. Fritjof Capra, *The Turning Point* (Toronto, New York: Bantam Books, 1982), p. 282.

Chapter 6

COORDINATING THE PADDLING

The Board of Directors

EVEN THOUGH NEW SOCIAL CHANGE GROUPS OFTEN START THROUGH the initiative of one person, they need quickly to evolve into shared leadership to maximize their wisdom, stability, and effectiveness. A coordinating committee of some kind becomes the place where tough decisions are confronted and policy is made. Groups that stabilize over time or grow beyond their founding circle need to find structures that work, including structures for setting policy. To strengthen themselves to deal with political struggles and an environment that resists social change, they need clarity about expectations, agreements, and rules.

Groups that do not have boards can benefit from the clarity of expectations and agreements discussed here. We describe a board of directors structure because there are specific points to be made about boards, as well as general points about organizational governance.

An organization incorporated as a nonprofit must by law have a board of directors. Legally, the nonprofit board represents the public trust, ensuring that the organization's resources are handled with care and that its mission is served effectively and within the limits of the law.

Boards can be a bane or a blessing. Boards can provide direction and wisdom, raise money, serve as a monitor and evaluator of the organization's performance, and be crucial in strategic planning. Boards can also try to micromanage the organization, get mired in staff power struggles, or forget to hold the director accountable until after the organization has run over a cliff. Boards are more likely to be a blessing when they are clear about their job and their boundaries, and when their individual members are clear about what they are doing there.

Responsibilities of a Board of a Nonprofit Organization

Determine the organization's mission and purposes.
The mission statement serves as a guide to everything the organization does and helps in setting priorities among competing demands.

Select and hire the chief staff person (or persons, if there is a top management team).
Possibly the most far-reaching of the board's responsibilities, this includes developing the job description and defining the role to be played (i.e., whether the chief staff person will be the chief executive officer (CEO) or the chief operating officer (COO). A CEO acts as the organizational leader and spokesperson, while a COO is an administrator working with the board chair who carries the CEO role). As an organization grows, this role often changes in practice without the change being recognized in the bylaws. As a result conflicting expectations often arise between board members and the chief staff person.

Support and evaluate the chief staff person.
In order to perform well and grow in the job, the person responsible for the daily operation of the organization needs feedback both in terms of what is going well, and where there is room for improvement. The chief staff person also should be asked for feedback on the board's functioning.

Ensure effective organizational planning.
Even though the organization's staff will often gather the necessary information and develop the actual planning documents, the board must be involved in setting direction and approving goals, objectives, and major operating policies. The board's most valuable role in the

planning process may be to ask questions and to ensure that the program supports the organization's mission.

Ensure adequate resources.
Even though fundraising, such as grantwriting, is often delegated to staff, the board is responsible for ensuring that the organization has the resources needed to carry out its mission. Many organizations expect board members to participate directly in fundraising through special events, solicitations, or by helping to open doors to potential funders. When this is the case, potential board members should be told of this expectation.

Ensure that resources are effectively managed.
This includes approving the annual budget and carefully reviewing regular financial reports, ensuring that the proper reports and taxes are filed with necessary government agencies, and authorizing the annual audit and reviewing (and understanding) the audit report. Inattention and carelessness in this area can get both the organization and individual board members in legal trouble.

Determine and monitor programs and services.
Since needs usually outstrip existing resources, the board's role is to ensure that the organization does what it says it is going to do and conducts high quality and cost-effective programs.

Ensure that necessary policies are in place, up-to-date and in effect.
Examples of such policies are bylaws, personnel policies, fee structures, conflict of interest policies, and risk management policies.

The bylaws should spell out lines of accountability between the board and the chief staff person. They will also determine whether the organization has formal members with voting rights, how the board is established and renewed over time, and by what rules the organization will make its decisions. The board is responsible for seeing that the organization operates within its own bylaws and in accordance with its articles of incorporation.

Other policies, such as personnel policies, are designed to ensure clear expectations of responsibilities and benefits and to establish

83

procedures for dealing with conflicts. A board that has not paid sufficient attention to the organization's personnel policies could put the organization at risk of an employment-related lawsuit.

Ensure compliance with local, state, and federal laws and regulations.
This responsibility runs through all of the board's work. Although board members cannot be expected to know about all legal matters that have to do with the group's operations, they must ask questions to make sure that competent legal advice is sought when necessary and that management is in compliance with relevant regulations. There may be times when a board will decide, as a matter of conscience, to oppose particular laws and refuse to go along with them, but that should be done with full consideration of the possible consequences, not out of carelessness.

Enhance the organization's public image.
In order to ensure constitutent support for the work of the organization and attract money for its programs, the board must see that effective informational materials are prepared and distributed and positive relationships are developed with others in the community. Each board member serves as a link to the larger constituency, but no board member, except the board chair, speaks for the organization unless specifically authorized to do so. Each board member is expected to feed back to the organization what they learn about constituent impressions of the group's work.

Ensuring board continuity and responsiveness.
There are no laws spelling out how boards are to be elected, but this should be a standard part of each group's bylaws. Whatever process has been selected, the board is responsible for seeing that it has at all times at least the minimum number of members and that the bylaws are followed regarding meetings, terms, and elections. Organizational leaders should consider what skills and perspectives are needed on the board and whether there is sufficient turnover to allow new ideas and fresh insights.[1]

Fulfill the responsibilities of individual board members.
Even though nonprofit board members are unlikely to be held

personally responsible for actions of their organizations, they are not totally invulnerable. Three legal standards apply. The duty of care requires that a board member exercise reasonable care in the conduct of her or his responsibilities, such as attending meetings, reading minutes, carefully reviewing financial statements, and asking questions to clarify issues. (Not attending is no excuse.) The duty of obedience requires that the board member's actions be guided by the organization's mission. The duty of loyalty requires a board member to refrain from conflicts of interest. We live in a society of conflicts and lawsuits. All boards ought to review their policies and practices periodically to guard against possible legal action against the organization or individual members.

Board Operations

Create a balanced board

It pays to have an active nominating committee, which identifies board needs, looks for and cultivates potential board members, and recommends new appointments. The same committee recommends current members for possible additional terms. There are many useful ways of thinking about balance in a board: skills, diversity of background and perspective, etc.

We propose the "3 W's": work, wealth, and wisdom. As a whole, the board needs to have some people who can work hard, some people who are seasoned and have the perspective which comes from experience, and some people with money. No one individual needs all three W's; the point is to get a balance.

The workers will often be people who have a specific concern or skill in one area of your work, which is fine; watch out, however, for people who are so attached to their speciality that they value only their own agenda. Before asking them to join the board, be sure they can appreciate the value of work they are not personally doing.

The wise ones have become so by reflecting on a range of experiences. The danger here is that they may develop some allergy to new ideas and experiments, wanting to interpret new proposals as "things we've tried before." Be sure that they have some openness and flexibility.

The third "W"—wealth—is a relative concept. A poor people's

85

> *To my chagrin I once learned the importance of consulting with individual board members when an important program proposal floundered because a powerful board member felt slighted that I, as the executive director had not discussed the idea with him prior to presenting it to the board. The proposal was in an area where the board member had a particular expertise. He later told me that he actually agreed with the proposal once he thought about it. The incident reminded me that board members have the same human needs for recognition as do staff members and everyone else. As I worked on formulating the proposal I had been thinking of 'the board' as a collective entity and overlooked the individuality of the members.*
>
> —former director of a group working against racism on a city level

organization may have some board members whose income puts them securely in the middle class. Why "wealthy" board members? Voluntary organizations often have cash flow problems which they interpret with a scarcity mentality: "We never have enough money." "There's not enough of anything around here." This easily becomes a self-fulfilling prophecy; a scarcity mentality is very close to the attitude of a loser, and most funding sources don't like to give to losers. Someone whose personal finances are sufficient (or even abundant) often is free from this haunting sense of lack, so she or he can hold out the perspective of "enough" in the organization. Of course, you won't want to give someone undue weight in decision-making because of their personal wealth or income.

Another reason for having some board members who are well-off is that people with money usually know other people with money, and they can ask them for contributions. All board members, whether poor, rich, or in between, need to take responsibility for fundraising if the organization is to flourish. Wealthier members, however, will often bring in more funds because of who they know.

Money is not the only measure of resources valuable to the organization. Wealth includes in-kind donations, barter, and shared use of property. We focus on money here because it is a particularly challenging issue for many activists.

> *In a fundraising workshop for board and volunteers, the trainer focused on the upcoming major donor campaign. "In a subtle way our job as fundraisers gets undermined by a feeling that there simply isn't enough money around, even though we know objectively that the people we're asking do have money to give away. The belief in our own heads about scarcity can get in the way of feeling free to ask for large gifts."*
>
> *"During the campaign," she suggested, "carry more cash in your purse or wallet than you normally would, to give yourself a sense of abundance."*
>
> *Hoots of laughter from several participants greeted the suggestion. "I don't have any extra money to carry in my purse!" The trainer was persistent, suggesting that money being saved for the next family birthday present could be carried, or grocery money or some of the rent money. More laughter followed each suggestion, and strenuous protest that even a few dollars could be found to put in the wallet. The trainer moved on to another subject in the workshop.*
>
> *The fundraising campaign failed, and the organization continued to be as hand-to-mouth as the members who couldn't imagine having a few extra dollars in their pocket.*
>
> —a consultant who worked with the organization

Take the time you need

Another area in which the scarcity mentality shows up in organizations is time. How to get nine to twenty board members together regularly, and spend enough time together to make sound decisions?

Aware that board members are volunteers, some board leaders or staff create a double standard in their minds: "It's OK for me to take a lot of time for this work, but I can't expect other people to do that." Another self-fulfilling prophecy! In these organizations the typical pattern is monthly board meetings of two to three hours, in which some people arrive late, others leave early, it takes thirty minutes to get rolling, and everyone ends up frustrated that the business didn't get done.

Try something different: regular, but less frequent, meetings of a half day or a whole day. Design them creatively, with the use of subgroups and high-participation techniques, for maximum productivity. Members can engage with each other where they are excited—their politics, their reading of what's happening in society as it bears on the issue, their strategic sense. The meeting will have a different quality from simply hearing staff reports or rubber stamping staff recommendations: a sense of progress will develop at each meeting.

When a member joins the board it needs to be made clear what participation is expected. Successful, high-energy organizations generally have a high level of participation from their boards, including attendance at meetings.

Establish an executive committee of the board (perhaps four or five people) which meets more often than the whole board, and give to it the authority to make emergency decisions and handle nonpolicy matters that do not need the whole board. Make sure the minutes are circulated to the board, and review them for approval by the board at its next meeting, so the executive committee does not get out of touch.

Choose the board size which matches your mission and constituencies

There is no standard size for a board. It depends on the resources you need and the number of constituencies that may need to be represented on the board. Resources include:

- skills and knowledge (writing, planning, finances, legal, group process, etc.)
- experience (with the issues, other boards, or similar groups)
- perspectives (related to race, class, gender, sexual orientation, politics, and other life experiences)
- access to financial support

In short, work, wisdom and wealth! However, don't assume that a lawyer board member will want to offer legal skills to your organization. She or he may like to volunteer for other tasks. Tell prospective board members what the board is seeking and ask them if it is something they are willing to give.

Regarding constituencies, remember that board members often provide legitimacy with various groups. Have someone on the board who is respected by each of your key allies (labor, religious, environmental, etc.).

Even though it's important to have a board that is diverse in terms of skills, experience, and connections, resist the temptation to put everyone on the board. A board larger than twenty-five may have trouble making timely decisions. On the other hand, a board smaller than nine or ten is unlikely to give you the diversity and people power you need.

One way to involve more people in ongoing work is to use non–board members on some of the board committees. This strengthens the work of the board, makes use of special skills and interests, and grooms people for future board membership.

Nurture strong board leadership

Establish coordination and cooperation between the board chair and the chief staff person in preparing board agendas and distributing information. Make sure that board meetings are facilitated well, with attention to group process as well as the agenda. The board chair does not have to facilitate meetings; that role can be rotated or delegated. If the board chair is strongly advocating a certain direction for the organization, someone else can facilitate the meetings to encourage balance and fairness. Cochairs and vice chairs are also possible as ways of delegating the facilitator role to someone other than a strong political leader who may not be the most appropriate facilitator.

Start accountability at the board level

In organizations where board members are not accountable to anyone, tensions between staff and board are chronic (although often suppressed). Further, within the board itself, needless tensions arise when members don't play their roles adequately. Try this: give a subcommittee responsibility for regular evaluation of board members (this could be the nominating committee). The committee makes certain that board membership expectations are clear and that there is an evaluation process for each individual, either yearly or when they are up for re-election.

Create a process which is simple and provides an opportunity for troubleshooting. For example, if you have a board member others see as aggressively pursuing his or her narrow agenda, through the evaluation process you can give feedback to the member and assist him or her to become a more effective member of the team. Some

One justice and peace group decided, after deliberation, to distribute leadership functions in an unusually clear way. The group elected a member of the board as president and gave him the job of spokesperson to the broader public. Another member was elected chair of the board, and her job was to keep track of the well-being of the organization itself, including the health of the board. Facilitation of board meetings was done by the board chair, who had strong skills as a facilitator. Larger coalition meetings were attended by the president, who also spoke at news conferences, published statements in the paper, and so on. Both the president and chair served on the personnel committee, which held yearly evaluations of the executive director, served as a sounding board for the executive director in personnel issues and was available for backup mediation in staff disputes. This arrangement used the skills of the three top leaders to best advantage and reduced the isolation which executive directors often feel in hierarchical organizations.

—former executive director of the organization

groups ask all board members to respond in writing to a few questions about how they see their own work and plans for the future.

Increasingly, both funding sources and advisors of nonprofits point to the importance of high-quality board performance and recommend or require regular assessments of the board. Every year or two, depending on the frequency of board meetings, a board ought to schedule a thorough assessment of how well it is meeting its responsibilities. A board assessment is likely to be more productive if it is facilitated by a skilled outsider. Don't be surprised if additional work surfaces from the assessment.

To consider whether assistance from a skilled consultant might enhance the effectiveness of your board at this time, here is a checklist:

- Is your board a group of people who are all working toward the same goals?
- Is there ongoing board education related to the issues the group is working on?
- In your organization, does the head of the board work effectively with the chief staff person?
- Does your board engage in long-term, strategic planning and evaluation?

- Does your board have an accurate picture of the group's financial situation?
- Does your board assess its own effectiveness on a regular basis and take action to make desirable improvements?
- Is there sufficient diversity of background and perspective on your board to challenge established views and avoid short-sighted decisions?
- Does service on your board provide its members with the personal satisfaction of making a difference?
- Do your board and committee meetings inform and involve their participants while also leading to timely decision-making?
- In their meetings, do members listen to each other and examine their own as well as others' assumptions?
- Is conflict on your board acknowledged and dealt with, rather than being allowed to fester and weaken the board's effectiveness?
- Are new board members well informed about your organization's mission and what will be expected of them before accepting nomination to serve?
- Do new board members receive adequate orientation at the beginning of their service?

If you answered "no" to a number of these questions, now might be a good time to take corrective action.

Increase clarity through orientation and training

Because many board members are engaged in a wide variety of activities, a critical yet often-overlooked area is orientation and training of new members. Over time, the result is that individuals who have been there the longest and know the ins and outs of the organization tend to gain an inordinate amount of control and influence. This can be resented by talented new members and can result in failure to use their skills fully. Any board needs to have an extensive, carefully thought-out orientation for new members. It may not, of course, be accomplished in just one session.

At a minimum, include in your orientation your group's bylaws and history, current programs, and budget; issues facing the organization at this point; an outline of board responsibilities and expectations; a list of board members; and an organizational chart with the names of key staff members.

Discover the best way to orient your board through experimentation. Experienced members might orient new members around particular areas of interest or expertise. Alternatively, a buddy system can assist new members to feel immediately supported and involved in activities where they initially may not feel comfortable, like fundraising or public speaking. New members need to read background information and historical data, and they could interview older members or the founders. (Some activists forget the strength and perspective which comes from knowing their roots.)

Board members are often assumed to know a lot, which they have not necessarily learned through experience. Break the expectation that members already know what they need to know by setting up a board training program. Create the expectation that members apprentice with experts, read books and materials, and attend seminars or training programs in order to be more effective in carrying out their particular tasks.

Define the board's authority

Confusion about the domain of a board's authority can be just as destructive as a confusion of roles in other aspects of life. Boards are established to maintain some level of objectivity about how organizations operate and whether or not they are meeting their established goals. Most boards, therefore, need to focus on establishing and maintaining policies, rather than getting involved, as a board, in operations.

How does the turf get confused? In small organizations with only one or a few paid staff members, members of the board also help implement the group's strategy. Board members may lead demonstrations, organize conferences, or do research. This arrangement can work fine, meeting the group's needs for skillful volunteers and meeting individual board members' interest in taking action. The arrangement also lends itself to problems. When controversies emerge about political direction, it's tempting for a board member to plunge into operations in order to make sure the organization is carrying out her or his point of view. When the board member is older, more experienced, or more influential than staff members (as is often the case), the staff can feel overwhelmed and unable to relate to the volunteer work of the board member in a straight forward way.

A major casualty in confusion of turf is accountability. This confusion happens in large organizations as well as small ones. How can a board member's volunteer operational work (as distinct from board work) be made accountable to staff, as other volunteers' work is?

A different pattern relating to turf is for board members to remain distant from the ongoing work of the organization until they see a special need or an emergency comes up. Then, like the Lone Ranger, they leap to the rescue, only to disappear once again. This behavior can create dependency, passivity, frustration, and hostility among the organization's staff members and volunteers, who tend to resent the rescue operation and the implied authority of board members in their area of responsibility.

Accept that the normal state of affairs between the board and the staff is dynamic tension. When you experience the tension, resist the temptation to lay blame or start a crusade; accept it as normal.

Insist on the principle that board members serving in operational roles are acting as volunteers, not board members, and have no special privileges. It is only when functioning as part of the board that board members have decision-making power. They have no special privileges or authority as individuals outside meetings of the board and its committees except as specifically delegated by the board. The executive director needs to back up staff members who are working with and holding accountable board members acting as volunteers. The board chair needs to back up the executive director, if it comes to that.

If a board member finds it difficult to play only one role at a time, it is better for her or him to choose whether to continue as board member, or to enjoy the volunteer work. If these principles are built into the orientation of board members and reclarified from time to time, a clear basis exists for working out the conflicts.

"Most organizations are run by the staff anyway, so why pay attention to the board?" This often-heard observation accepts diminished power for the organization. A board's wisdom, stability, fundraising, planning smarts, and place of accountability are important resources. The board also can represent the constituency of the organization and reduce the chance that high-powered staff will, over time, lose touch. We hope in this chapter that we've shown specific, practical ways you can get the most benefit from an active board or coordinating committee. They all come down to one thing: clarity of expectations and agreements.

Notes

1. A more detailed description of board legal responsibilities can be found in the pamphlet by Jacqueline Covey Leifer and Michael B. Glomb, *The Legal Obligations of Nonprofit Boards: A Guidebook for Board Members* (Washington: National Center for Nonprofit Boards, 1993). This center has a wide range of publications about specific board related issues.

Chapter 7

RECOGNIZING AND SHARING LEADERSHIP

Dealing with Issues of Authority and Control

RAFTING ON A RIVER IS A LOT SAFER—AND A LOT MORE FUN—IF companions work out ahead of time who decides what, when. Which rules are chosen for the trip may be less important than clarity in choosing them. Leaving leadership questions unanswered often leads to resentment, alienation, and even an overturned raft.

Be straightforward about issues of authority and control. Clarify what decision-making roles your organization needs. Invest the people in those roles with the authority to make decisions. This is different from influence, or informal leadership. You have influence if people take your opinions seriously; you have authority if you have the right to make certain kinds of decisions. Most organizations place authority for making policy and deciding legal matters with the board while operational authority is vested in the staff.

In this chapter we focus on one function of authority: coordinating the work. Every successful group needs as least one person to think about the whole and coordinate its parts. This function may be carried out by a collective rather than an individual. If the organization designates this function to a chair, executive director, or staff collective, we call it authoritative leadership. This chapter is addressed to those authorized to make decisions on behalf of the organization, whether executive director, staff collective, board, or whole membership.

> The staff in the social justice department of our denomination got excited about the concept of collective, so we became a team without a director. It went great: productivity and morale increased. The one person who put out less work was Ann, who was greatly enjoying the new structure. She was doing OK productivity-wise, so there was no pressure to replace her. I don't think any of us understood her role until Ann moved two years later to another part of the country. A few months later, with unresolved problems piling up, I reflected on what it was Ann really did while she was away from her desk chatting with us all and running across the hall to visit with the overall administration of the denomination. I thought she, outgoing personality that she was, was simply "relating." In fact, she was coordinating, troubleshooting, resolving interpersonal tensions, gathering and processing agenda items for our collective meetings, heading off trouble from the administration. Only in her absence did I understand that a successful team needs at least one person to think about the whole group, even if that's only done informally. Strategic thinking might happen fine in meetings, but maintainence of a successful team needs a lot more than meetings!
>
> —a Quaker peace activist

Individuals and Authority

Be honest with yourself about how you maintain your power. There are qualities that add to your influence other than additional authority, such as expertise, conflict resolution skills, or charisma (in some cultural traditions). Ask yourself: "Do I maintain power by witholding information from others that they could reasonably and responsibly use?" "Do I avoid defining the limits of my (or our team's) authority?"

Controlling information and access to it is an age-old practice. Less widely understood is the second problem that arises in organizations: vague and changing limits of authority. It's common for leaders* never to define how much authority they have, and therefore always to be in a position to take what they think they need. Others

---

* For convenience in writing, we refer to "leaders" or "the leader;" who could be a manager, board chair, executive director, team coordinator, board of directors, or other individual or group with authority.

are left dangling, unable to know whether they have the authority to do what's called for in a particular situation.

Imagine authority being divided into that used directly by the leader, that shared between the leader and others, and that delegated to an individual or committee. Each of these three areas of authority can be larger or smaller, depending on the trust of the leader and others in the organization, the maturity of the other units, the types of tasks or problems being tackled, and organizational structure.

Organizations often fail to define the authority of their leaders. Left vague, the authority exercised by the leader will vary depending on his or her willingness to share responsibility with others. This "window of authority" will vary in size almost as if there were a windowshade which could be drawn down or let up at the discretion of the leader. If the leader sees things going well, she or he will raise the shade and let more authority be shared. But if the situation is difficult or trust is in short supply, the windowshade is drawn down and the authority of other units is restricted.

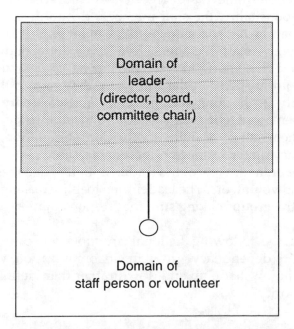

WINDOW OF AUTHORITY WITH WINDOWSHADE

97

Leaders typically hold on to more authority than they need, "just in case." This is self-defeating because the authority a leader doesn't need most of the time, other people do need to do their work in the most effective manner possible. Activist work often requires timeliness: getting coalition spokespeople lined up quickly for a news conference, calling a demonstration to respond to police brutality, getting a grant proposal in before the deadline. If staff or committees are unsure whether they can act quickly and decisively, valuable time is lost and impact is reduced.

To understand fully the windowshade effect, we need to watch an organization over time. A leader moves the shade up and down depending on the situation and her or his own levels of anxiety and trust at any given moment in time. Other units in the organization (program staff, for example) learn quickly that the key to success is not to disappoint the leader, because to do so would reduce their ability to act or the degree to which they are given responsibility. A subtle game begins to occur. While the leader looks out through the window of authority to determine the degree to which she or he is willing to delegate responsibility, the staff member tries to discover "what the boss wants" and what success would mean for him or her. A collusion occurs in which staff members give away independent thinking, creativity, and risk taking in return for being acceptable to the boss. Eager to avoid mistakes in the short run, they reduce their initiative and creativity in the long run: initiative and creativity can flourish only in an environment where it is OK to take risks and to make mistakes. The result is declining motivation, stimulation, and interest, as dependency on the authority figure increases.

From the point of view of the leader, initiative declines among staff members and volunteers. The leader then feels increasingly inclined to hover over the group making sure that responsibilities are carried out "just right."

Through the following fictional anecdote we can see one way passivity and dependency grow in an organization when leaders move the windowshade up and down rather than defining the limits of their authority.

Maria, the chair of a small housing action organization, asked Jo to organize the October fundraising drive. Jo gave an enthusiastic "yes," seeing this as a chance to impress Maria, do something useful for the organization, and extend her own skill level. She attacked the project with vigor. Proud of her progress two weeks later, she reported back to Maria to review the project to date.

"Jo, you've really jumped into this project; I wish more people around here had your enthusiasm," Maria began. She then went on to ask, "Have you thought about...?" "If I were you, I would think seriously about... "I like this, but you might want to consider...." "In my experience, I've found it useful to..."

The longer the meeting went, the more deflated and depleted Jo felt. What Maria thought was helpful advice was experienced by Jo as second-guessing that showed Maria's lack of confidence in her. Maria was backseat-driving! If Maria knew all this information, why didn't she share it in her briefing at the beginning of the project? By the end of the meeting, Jo trudged out to complete the project out of obligation rather than enthusiasm; it no longer felt like Jo's project, but something she was doing for Maria.

Maria probably thought she was coaching rather than being a "boss." From the point of view of Jo, Maria gave Jo both responsibility for the fundraising drive and the authority to make the needed decisions, and then in the meeting took the authority back, despite the soft rhetoric of suggestions rather than orders.

Removing the moveable shade from the authority window means defining the authority clearly, including its limits. Removing the windowshade enables delegating genuine authority to others. Develop a clear and widely shared understanding of where the authority of each unit begins and ends in relation to the critical issues and projects of the organization. Put in writing where the authority of the leader ends as well as begins. The more authority and control a leader can give up, the more influence she or he generally will be able to attain. This does not mean giving up all one's authority—accountability, after all, requires some authority.

The amount of authority and control given to staff members and volunteers depends largely on the complexity of the task and the individual's readiness to take it on. In the short run, it is easier to tell someone what to do and how to do it than to take the time to delegate a project, establish the boundaries of your own authority so they know it really is their project, create an effective process of accountability, and make yourself available for coaching. It is tempting, but the cost of thinking only of the short term may be dependency, lack of initiative and creativity, low morale, and internal power struggles.

Coaching provides a way for a leader to relate to a staff member or volunteer who needs direction, support, and suggestions. How much direction and support is given at any time is one of the judgment calls coaches need to make. The more the staff member can be coached into asking the tough questions on the job, clarifying criteria for success, and laying out plans that can be openly discussed, the less the leader has to do it for them. There's a natural balancing act in the relation between leader and staff member; good coaching is understanding how much information and advice must be provided in relation to each task.

If you have been drawing the windowshade up and down and want to change that dynamic, start by explaining your past practice. Invite your team to assist you in changing by asking, each time a task is coordinated, what the responsibilities and authority going with the task are, how success will be measured, how the task will be supervised, and what your role will be as coordinator and coach.

Staff and committee meetings are opportunities for nurturing clear boundaries. At the beginning of the meeting, clarify each agenda item by asking if a decision is needed, who will make the decision, and what type of action needs to be taken. On some issues, the leader needs the advice and counsel of the group before making a decision. On other issues, the group itself may decide. Raising these questions at the beginning of each meeting empowers staff or committee members to clarify their own participation and even to question where the decision should be made; they demystify where authority lies in the organization.

It's often the case that a group has internal disagreements about how its decision-making structure should operate. Members can usually live with a structure they disagree with, deciding either to work to change the structure over time or to accept it while giving priority to other areas of work. What hurts morale is a covert and inconsistent structure, where a windowshade is drawn up and down and those not in leadership are left hanging.

A leader is frequently faced with the dilemma that people want her or him to make a decision and hold on to the authority so that they will not have to face the possible consequences of making the decision. This can be exacerbated when operating in crisis mode, which seems to demand immediate decisions and solutions. It is easy for leaders who are bright, quick, and motivated by a sense of urgency to be tacitly expected to take on more authority in such situations than is necessary.

People may be uncomfortable with shared authority when mistakes or wrong choices can have negative consequences. The reality is that growing in our power and competence usually means operating outside our comfort zone—beware of protecting people from discomfort and maintaining their dependency. Consider:

- Increasing authority has been proven to be a much greater morale booster and reward than increasing wages. Rod Napier has found that soon after wages are increased staff members tend to see themselves as having deserved the increase, and therefore the raise was a matter of simple justice.[1]
- Shared leadership means shared ownership of consequences, both the high of success and the low of failure. Every organization has its tough times, which are much tougher when people scapegoat a leader instead of owning the problems together.
- Increased authority and responsibility yields more initiative and creativity, both of which are critical for success in social change. Because social change happens in what consultants call a turbulent environment, rigid or centralized authority is actually dysfunctional.[2]
- As a leader your role can shift from the harried manager trying to get people to do what you would do with their task, to a coordinator of projects and a coach of people, supporting them to do the work.

Steering Committees and Problem Solving

Ask yourself if problems are cropping up faster than you can solve them. There are times in every organization's life when problems seem to multiply like rabbits. No matter how many hours the director works, no matter how much the board chair worries, problems clamor for attention. The stress of this white-water condition often makes leaders feel they need to take more control, while others complain about the demands made on them but take little responsibility for dealing with the problems. As leaders become less flexible and others have less autonomy, organizational democracy suffers and problems keep growing.

If you're wise you know there's nothing wrong with having problems. Problems are like weights are to the weightlifter. As we tackle problems we get stronger. When the problems fly at us faster than we can handle them, we need to increase our organizational capacity for problem solving. One democratic, participatory way of doing this is through a steering committee.

You may know the term *steering committee* from other organizations where it is used to describe a group that leads or "steers" the organization, functioning more or less like a board or an executive committee. As you will see, that is not the way we use the term in this chapter.

Create a steering committee to prioritize and facilitate problem solving. A steering committee does not take the place of the board, executive director, staff collective, or other leadership structures, because its job is not to make substantive decisions. The steering committee collects issues, concerns, opinions, data, information, and ideas and sends them to the right places. It prioritizes the problems to reduce overload. It is a clearing-house open to all parts of the organization, especially those most alienated. It is the answer to the complaint: "I can't get the director or board to pay attention to this!"

Elect the steering committee in a representative way. The typical steering committee consists of five to twelve members, depending on the size and complexity of your organization or work unit. Members are elected by staff members and volunteers in a way that represents the breadth of the organization. One committee position is for the director or designee. The board also may be represented. They need to be elected not as power brokers but for their wisdom and good sense, since their role on the steering committee involves delegation and organization much more than power and influence.

The group will meet regularly (how often will depend on the size of the organization and complexity of the problems) to talk about the issues that are blocking the organization's effectiveness in operating or in reaching its goals. Before it starts its work, the group needs a training session on its mission, group dynamics, holding effective meetings, and rules and procedures. Steering committee members must understand their roles and figure out effective ways to get their tasks accomplished.

Physicist Fritjof Capra uses the metaphor of a tree to describe an organization: both the leaves and the roots provide nourishment. Trees grow through energy transfers upward and downward, just as organizations do. An organization overwhelmed with problems experiences separation between leaves and roots: leaders become out of touch, and staff and members become alienated. The steering committee is like the trunk of a healthy tree, maintaining the flow of energy between the parts.

Let the steering committee prioritize, gather information, and decide who will decide. The steering committee, representative of the whole organization, is in a strategic place to make judgement calls about which problems take priority. It can take an active role in gathering problems and ideas for solution through interviewing, questionnaires, or open discussion. Its meetings can be open to the general membership if it wishes. The steering committee also identifies the most appropriate groups or individuals within the organization to generate options for how to deal with the issues at hand.

Once possible solutions have been generated, the steering group decides who is to decide. Should it be the decision of the director, the board, a particular department or subgroup, or the whole organization? If it is a group decision, the steering committee also decides what decision-making method to use. Another part of the steering committee's work is to keep track of progress. It monitors the status of the problems sent off to be solved: Is the problem-solving unit stuck? Is it time to evaluate a solution that was implemented last year?

These process decisions by the steering committee need at least a minimum of trust by the whole organization, which is why the committee is elected in a representative way. If it does its work well, as bottlenecks are eased and solutions are found the trust level rises.

To keep the trust of the organization, the steering committee must

103

remember that it is not solving problems for the organization. Instead, it is taking the pulse of the organization and facilitating problem solving. Members of the committee may have good ideas and potential solutions, so they will be tempted to solve problems themselves. Yielding to this temptation turns the committee into a decision-making group, undermines credibility, and complicates lines of accountability and leadership within the organization.

Try rotating the membership of the steering committee after one- or two-year terms, staggering the terms so there is continuity as well as turnover. Rotation builds credibility by giving more people a chance to participate and reduces the temptation to stray from the job of facilitating rather than making decisions.

Use the steering committee for ongoing organizational development. Usually an organization will create a steering committee to deal with an immediate problem. The best time to create a steering committee is when your organization is not in the middle of a crisis, although any time is better than never. Since every organization has problems that need to be attended to, a steering committee can help prevent a buildup as well as dissolve bottlenecks. Having a mechanism through which members can identify problem areas and suggest solutions improves morale and protects against leaks in the raft. You'll find that an ongoing steering committee can assist in many key areas of organizational development:

- Internal organization: Job design, organization of work units, and organizational change
- Human resources: Staff selection processes, performance appraisal design, staff development, and pay, benefit, and incentive plans
- Leadership: Feedback on style and impact of leadership and work climate assessment
- Operations: Policy and procedure development and review, and improvement of organizational communications
- Control: Methods of accountability and monitoring, quality control, process and outcome evaluations, and work task assignment

Don't forget to enjoy the benefits of a well-functioning steering committee. With a well-functioning steering committee there is time to relax. Notice the following concrete benefits to the organization: More and better data. Two-way communication between leaders and staff. Commitment and involvement of members. Improved efficiency and effectiveness. Higher productivity. Fewer grievances and absenteeism. Less tardiness and turnover. A better work climate. Best of all, a better chance to achieve your organization's goals!

Notes

1. Another good source is Marvin R. Weisbord, *Productive Workplaces: Organizing and Managing for Dignity, Meaning and Community* (San Francisco: Jossey-Bass, 1987).
2. For an in-depth discussion of this, see Gareth Morgan, *Images of Organization* (Newbury Park, Calif.: Sage, 1986), chapter 2.

Chapter 8

MAPPING THE JOURNEY

Incorporating Strategic Planning

Take charge by planning or drift into eddies that go nowhere. Our discussion of organizational growth from primary to secondary systems showed how growth is less painful if you intentionally adopt a process and implement it. If you grow, or if your organization is staying around for the long haul, it's easy to drift into bureaucratic forms.

This chapter discusses a dynamic process of planning which is democratic, participatory, and creative, in which you work with your most active members to clarify the group's values, mission, and vision, create a plan, and create feedback mechanisms so your plan stays lively, flexible, and "in tune" with the changing situation.

> **I see failure where organizations don't have a plan—or don't stick to it if they have it, reacting to events rather than stepping back to re-focus and adjust their plan.**
>
> *—long-time labor and community organizer*

Clarify Your Values

Outside forces like government and funders pressure us to conform to their values and, over time, are likely to affect a shift in values without the group noticing. Until recently, organizations rarely identified values or used them to guide their work, measure performance, or see if the organization was still on track. If we value open communications, we should be able to measure the degree to which people experience such communication within the group. If we value collaborative problem solving rather than top-down commands, we can measure whether that is happening. If we value diversity, there are measures available to see whether our daily practice reflects a diversity consciousness. Agree on criteria that measure what really matters most to you.

Values are the bedrock of all organizational policies. They form the foundation for the vision, mission, and goals of the group. By agreeing on value statements, we take the first step to reducing the credibility gap that opens when we don't "walk our talk." An example for a citywide organization that serves neighborhood groups might be: "Our programs and projects need to strengthen the bond between member groups and their grassroots constituents."

Clarify Your Mission

Use a direct and participatory process that helps everyone own the process of making your mission statement. The mission statement needs to be an essential part of the life of the organization, incorporating the key values and purposes that guide the organization in its decisions about both product and process.

We recommend a succinct picture (perhaps sixty words) of the organization's current reality:

- Who is the organization? What are its most important reasons for existing?
- What are its results or services that are most valued?
- What makes the organization unique?
- Who does it serve?
- What does it care about in how it relates to those it serves and to its own workforce?

You can use a mission statement as a framework for evaluating past work and for guiding future planning. The mission can change over time as the group changes and adapts to new realities.

Here's an example of a brief and inspiring mission statement from a local church congregation: "The aim of the people of St. John's is to be a community rooted in its relationship with God, and a beacon of hope within the world, where people are fed, supported, and connected."

Another example comes from the publisher of this book: "New Society Publishers is a not-for-profit, worker-controlled publishing house, dedicated to promoting fundamental social change through nonviolent action."

If there is already agreement on organizational values, ninety percent of the work in creating a mission statement can happen in three hours. We made up the following example to make the process transparent:

Neighbors Opposing Slimy Harbors (NOSH) grew from an ad hoc protest of sewage dumping to an ongoing group with an ecological vision. To create their mission statement, they pulled together their staff, board, and key volunteers—twenty-four people in all. Each individual took ten minutes to list a series of statements or ideas that they believed should be incorporated into a mission statement. Six groups of four were then formed, mixing up board, staff, and volunteers.

The groups were given ninety minutes to create a rough draft mission, drawing on the individuals' work. The facilitator suggested each group use the first thirty to forty minutes listing the individuals' statements on newsprint and discussing which ones had a lot in common and which unique ones added something others agreed was important. As it turned out, many of the individual statements did draw support, so the groups had an early sense of success. Someone in each group then led the effort to frame the various statements into a coherent whole. Participants were cautioned to do this in a constructive rather than competitive way. At the end of the ninety minutes each group's draft was placed on newsprint to be presented to a second group.

Now the six groups became three paired groups. Within the paired groups, each one presented their draft with the other group first asking only questions for clarification and noting commonalities. They had forty-five minutes to do this and to put together the best single draft mission statement they could, again on newsprint.

Next the whole group of twenty-four came together to review the three draft mission statements. The elements in common from the three drafts leapt out at the whole group, and there was time for comments and observations. Each of the three subgroups selected a person they felt could integrate the best of the three mission statements while the group took a dinner break. The three individuals took an hour to integrate the texts. After dinner the NOSH activists met and, after a brief discussion, agreed on their unified mission statement.

This process is dynamic, challenging, and intended to combine a high degree of participation and success in a short period of time.

To Build Inspiration, Create a Vision

The mission is a focused statement of your organization's present identity and reason for existing. The vision pictures where it wants to be in three to five years. It is not a pie-in-the-sky, idealistic view that cannot be reached. The vision is within the realm of possibilities, and reflects where the organization needs to go to further its potential. It may reflect expansion, growth and change, or the polishing and enhancing needed to increase organizational quality over time. Vision statements illuminate and stimulate to action.

One springboard to the vision is looking at the mission statement and asking: "What is missing from this picture? What should we be doing that we aren't? What are we doing that we shouldn't need to be doing down the road? What is changing out there that we aren't addressing now? What resources may become available? Which of our values could we be expressing more fully?"

Just as a mission offers a standard against which an organization can be measured in its present work, a vision statement can act as a guide and standard against which to measure an organization's success as it moves into the future. As with the mission statement, it should be short, sweet, and succinct, written in a way that is memorable, so it becomes a lively part of the organizational culture.[1]

Bring Others on Board

Face honestly and directly any resistance you may find to developing an organizational plan. The empowerment of a group as a whole requires planning. Without a plan, and a democratic process of creating it, the organization's future is determined by dominant members inside and dominant pressures outside. Knowing that doesn't mean there won't be strong resistance, however.

It can be difficult to understand why planning often meets strong foot dragging, especially if you personally think that planning is a very reasonable and sensible process.[2] People sometimes fear that planning:

- increases rigidity,
- leaves out intuition and creativity,
- is just for experts,
- results in reports that sit on dusty shelves and don't get implemented,
- is for national groups, because the job of local groups is to implement national strategies rather than devise their own,
- takes too much time,
- means prioritizing, which leaves out some projects, which leaves out some people.

These fears are taken into account in the steps suggested here. Planning should support flexibility rather than rigidity and use intuition and creativity in the process. Clear design and facilitation moves planning from the experts to the people. The plans that gather dust are usually done with too little input; only a few of the people really owned the result. Even when national movements have clear strategies, local groups need to devise strategies which take into account local circumstances and resources. Participatory planning does take time, but the resulting unity can save time in the long run by avoiding continuing power struggles over issues that can be settled in the planning process.

It's true that planning does mean prioritizing. The increased focus that results means the group will not be all things to all people. Making choices can be painful. It helps to compare it with the pain of not planning: confusion over goals and objectives, frustration that we're forever responding to crises, and a feeling of inadequacy because we never get our work done.

110

As the executive director of a new organization I wanted to get us off to the best start possible, and our leading funder said that required a very specific plan with measurable objectives. I came back to the office knowing he was right and yet feeling conflicted inside. As I sat in my office to start drafting the initial plan, I became more and more upset. My brain refused to work, while my stomach churned more and more. Finally I realized what was going on: if I laid out specific measurable objectives, I was going to be held accountable. I didn't want to be held accountable! I wanted to be credited for my good intentions and hard work and not criticized because we didn't achieve this or that particular thing. I had to sit with my upset feelings for quite a while before breaking through to a new place inside myself....I guess it was an ego thing that I had to get past, feeling like accountability means harsh criticism or attack of me as a person. Facing that upset was a maturing experience for me as an organizer. And I also realize that I was setting myself up even more for my negative reaction by trying to draft a set of objectives by myself instead of leading the group through a collective process.

—an experienced organizer who had led several organizations before having the experience recounted here

Because the dynamic of resistance will influence planning at every step, we recommend that you take some time to face it. After a brief presentation on what planning entails, try the following design:

- Brainstorm the advantages of planning, listing them on newsprint.
- Brainstorm the disadvantages of planning.
- Ask each person to identify which of the disadvantages is the most troublesome for her or him personally. Check those mentioned.
- Look at the disadvantages that have been checked, one at a time, brainstorming how that disadvantage could be handled. Look at the disadvantages as problems to be solved. An alternative would be to ask small groups of two or three to take the disadvantages to work on before the next meeting, bringing back proposals on how to solve them.
- Consider "What will happen if we don't plan?"

- Make a decision. If a large minority opposes planning, the group should decide to drop it or agree to discuss it again in half a year or a year.

Analyze the Relationship of Your Organization to Its Environment

Bill Moyer's Movement Action Plan (see chapter 1) is relevant to this piece of work. Is the organization part of a booming social movement? Is it just beginning to test the waters politically? Has the movement it is part of crested in terms of dramatic impact, and does the organization need to adjust to the new possibilities for implementation of change? How does this historical context affect the funding base and the potential of allies to give support? Are there politicians who want to use your issue to help them get elected? Are there global trends that will affect your cause one way or the other? These kinds of questions need to be asked so planning is genuinely strategic, rather than simply incremental or mechanistic.[3]

Use an Effective Planning Process

Allow the drama of planning to emerge through graphics and broad participation. The dramatic elements of planning are always needed to keep people's attention and energy. A skilled facilitator can work with a group of any size (board, staff, or volunteers) by organizing subgroups for particular tasks and bringing everyone together for debate of key choices and for building the big picture.

Choose a room where one wall can be devoted to the whole plan, to give yourselves enough room. Across the top are time intervals: in a four-year plan, the units might be three-month intervals. On the right side are listed the goals to be accomplished by the end of the four years. Working back from those outcomes to the present, asking ourselves what would have to be accomplished at each preceding step, we can begin to see what kinds of strategic events must occur if we are to succeed. Each strategic event itself becomes a goal, around which a strategy or series of strategies must be developed if success is to occur.

Because our organizations usually have a whole set of goals, the whole wall is needed in order to see the relationship between the goals and the sequence of events building up to their achievement. Just by looking, it becomes possible to see where to shift things around to ease the work load and cash flow—for example, not to have the major lobbying push happen at the same time as the biggest fundraising event, or the direct action campaign launch at the same time as a membership drive.

All plans, regardless of their complexity, have certain things in common. First, outcomes must be projected. Second, the critical events needed to reach the particular outcome must be identified. Third, the amount of time to accomplish the larger vision or outcome, as well as the developmental or intervening events, must be plotted on the overall timeline from beginning to end. Fourth, for each event along the way, resources and strategies must be allocated to ensure success.

A planning process can be as specific and complicated as needed. Be careful not to get lost in the plan itself! A plan shows goals that are reached through a series of specific objectives. These objectives are facilitated through key strategies and the strategies are accomplished through very particular tactics or actions. A plan is at best a vehicle for tracking events toward the goal and a guideline for allocation of resources.

Designing the most effective strategy planning process for your organization may need the assistance of a facilitator and a detailed handbook. *Thinking Strategically*, by Kehler, Ayvazian, and Senturia, a manual which grew out of a number of grassroots planning workshops, is a good place to start.

Implement the Plan, Collect Feedback, and Revise it at Intervals

The process of creating the plan often spotlights personnel (from staff, board, or volunteers) who have particular skills or interests in aspects of the plan, so be prepared to set up new task groups and structures to get things done. In this way, the planning process becomes a renewing and energizing force for the organization.

Another aspect of implementing the plan is supervision, because the best planning in the world doesn't work if the action steps aren't taken competently and with support. We deal with this complicated topic in a later chapter.

Managers need to gather a wide range of information and use it consistently to keep on track and re-evaluate the track the group is on. This data gathering does not require technical expertise. Most important is that organizational leaders ask the right questions to know the truth of any situation that demands action or a decision.

Some information is relatively objective: number of people

attending events; financial responses to newspaper ads; proportion of people of color, women, or other groups in the volunteer base; etc. The apparent simplicity of numbers, however, does not mean that you can safely rely on just one person to collect information. A second person to check the reasoning and methodology is often helpful. The classic case is the neighborhood organization which had a storefront for giving direct service. The receptionist was asked to keep track of how many people came during a given month, as a way of generating data on the clients served. A very impressive number was reached before someone noticed that a lot of passersby came into the building to use the bathrooms.

About data gathering, there is bad news and there is good news. The bad news is a leader may not get the truth simply by asking directly for it, especially if the truth is not happy. For a variety of reasons, including both respect and fear, participants may hold back on telling what they perceive is happening. Telling the truth about a situation has sometimes cost people dearly; it's sometimes known as "shooting the messenger." The good news about data gathering is that we can do it in a way that enables people to feel protected and that results in the consequences of their observations being constructive.

> I find that I learn more about what's happening in my staff if I'm aware that people need a bit of insulation. Either they protect themselves by withholding, or I protect them by the way I ask. For example, I'll say, "By the way, Joe, what's the grapevine say are the issues we should be dealing with?" or "What are people saying that management should be addressing and is somehow not getting done?" By giving people permission to speak for others, I'm giving the person I'm talking with the chance to be more honest and feel less vulnerable.
>
> —*a former school principal*

Five- or ten-minute casual interviews around a particular topic can provide an enormous amount of information quickly, without a lot of risk to those responding. In our experience, when individuals feel that their information is being heard and retribution is not part of the

114

response, the degree of openness and frankness to questions of real concern goes up dramatically.

Another way to take the pulse of the organization or to identify areas where it may be in strategic trouble is through brief one-page questionnaires that allow people to respond anonymously. If you explain why the information is important and that they will hear the results, they will be honest. A stimulating question, which nearly always brings valuable data, is: "If you were executive director, what are three things you would do immediately to improve our organization that I am not doing?" This question can be balanced by "What are three things I am doing right and should continue to do?" Or "What are three things that need to be said that are not being said in this organization at the present time?"

A variation is creating scaled items, which provide a sense of objectivity and subtlety. Sometimes people are uneasy with words, which may feel too extreme. For example:

On a scale of 1 to 10, to what degree is this organization dealing effectively with its conflicts?

1	5	10
Least		Most

If you responded at 6 or below, please indicate one or two areas of conflict you believe we should be addressing.

Another way to generate good feedback is using small groups during a meeting. This is a time-saving device that assists in staying on course and noticing areas where the plan needs changing. For example, if there are fifteen people in a meeting, put people in groups of three and ask the groups to take ten minutes to discuss each of three questions: "What are your ideas concerning our recent drop in volunteers?" "What specific suggestions would your group have as we enter this new phase of recruitment related to the fall campaign?" "What are your ideas for our annual party for volunteers that would make it celebratory, and playful, yet not lose focus on our reasons for existence?"

In a thirty-minute discussion, answers to these questions could provide the organization with important ideas, concerns and insights. The small group context also enhances the sense of community and personal empowerment.

Plans don't rigidify the organization if there are good feedback mechanisms in place, although these should not be overdone. There's the story of the youngster who pulled his new plant out of the flower pot each day and then replanted it. A friend noticed and asked why he did it. "Because I want to see how the roots are growing," he replied.

We don't recommend such steady scrutiny that your organization dies of observation. On the other hand, thoughtful data gathering often enables leaders to ward off an organizational crisis, reduce the impact of a problem, keep the organization on its strategic course, and flag the indicators that a shift in strategy makes sense.

Notes

1. Groups that face complex and controversial issues may find that taking extra time to orient themselves in the bigger picture of their field will make their five-year vision more persuasive and inspiring. A model for this is provided by the study-group visioning process by Robert A. Irwin, *Building a Peace System* (Washington, D.C.: ExPro Press, 1989).
2. This discussion of resistance draws on the manual *Thinking Strategically: A Primer on Long-Range Strategic Planning*, by Randall Kehler, Andrea Ayvazian, and Ben Senturia (Amherst, Mass.: Exchange Project, 1986).
3. In their manual on strategic planning, Kehler, Ayvazian, and Senturia explain that incremental (or mechanistic) planning simply organizes activities on a timeline without considering how they are linked and build on each other (or fail to build on each other). See *Thinking Strategically*.

PART III

STEERING THROUGH WHITE WATER

Here we share how successful organizations have learned day-to-day effectiveness. The strongest strategic plan is worthless if our staff and members are not implementing it and keeping track of implementation through meetings and supervision. Meetings and supervision, properly done, also provide feedback for changing the plan—key to success in the turbulent environment of most grassroots and nonprofit groups. The challenge of daily problem solving is easier to meet in groups with high morale, yet even high-spirited groups can benefit from a mechanism that specializes in getting problems handled.

Chapter 9

CREATING PRODUCTIVE MEETINGS

Planning the journey puts your group in a strong position to handle itself on the river of change. Implementing the plan requires meetings, times when the crew takes readings on where you are, makes course corrections, resolves conflicts, and clarifies who is doing what.

A good meeting is like a good campaign: careful planning and preparation results in variety, teamwork, and a clear strategy. A campaign that uses only one tactic, has campaigners competing with each other, and lacks a strategy is likely to fail. Designing a meeting is like preparing for the campaign: you want a cooperative spirit and a variety of activities that move the group toward its goals. If your team is used to mediocre meetings, you'll need to put extra time and energy into preparation. If these suggestions seem time-consuming, ask yourself what it's worth to become a more productive group.

Powerful meetings come from clear and obtainable goals. Create such goals for the meeting, and get agreement on them at the beginning. This may require finding ways to trim the agenda to the time available. When agreed-upon goals are on a chart on the wall, and the agenda listed beside it, you are setting up a situation for maximum productivity.

Develop process goals that help build cooperation and teamwork. What most people remember after a meeting, in addition to what they accomplished, is how they accomplished it, including their feelings about participation. Do people feel discounted and patronized, or do they feel valued and supported? An example of a process goal is to widen participation to include everyone.[1]

Designing an Agenda

Take time to plan the agenda, match it to the people who are coming, and find the right sequence.

You may know an organizer who spends many hours persuading people to come to meetings, but spends almost no time making sure the meetings feel worth coming to once the members are there. A four-hour board meeting of eighteen people equals seventy-two hours of "people time." That easily represents over $1,000 of value, and we wonder how many people would say, on their way home: "That meeting was worth $1,000." Most groups have tight budgets and are under financial strain. Doesn't it make sense that a $1,000 meeting should take at least a few hours of planning by more than one person?

Gear the agenda to the people, and the people to the agenda. At many meetings, the wrong people will attend for the wrong reasons. It's like suddenly asking a football team to grab instruments and join the band for the half-time festival. It might be interesting, but it won't be music. Resist the numbers game that sees a goal of getting lots of people into the room, whether or not they want to be there and have something to contribute. On the other hand, if you want to inspire lots of people to mobilize for your campaign, then don't design an agenda of business items that seem irrelevant and boring to most of them. Match the agenda to the attenders.

If you find that clusters of individuals continually gravitate toward each other or express opinions together, and your goal is to create a more broad-based consensus within the group, design the meeting with that in mind. Randomize the small groups, for example, and find other ways of mixing people and assisting them to find new things in common and new points of difference.

Orchestrate the agenda for maximum effectiveness. Gather agenda items well in advance. Give the leader a chance to contribute to but not to determine, the whole agenda. Create a representative agenda committee, rotating periodically, that solicits and screens agenda items. In some groups where an executive committee meets between board meetings, the executive committee creates the agenda. In these ways you are likely to create an agenda that really is appealing or important to the members.

When you are putting items in order, consider what will assist the group. If members are feeling discouraged, a couple of quick and easy

The coalition meeting in the Methodist Church basement was called for neighborhood leaders to consider organizing a fair. The neighborhood had been sliding downhill and needed a boost, and a fair might build unity. The initiative came from a small team of peace people who wanted to protest the building of an expensive new weapons system, and they had figured out how much tax money would be drawn from the area to build it—a mind-boggling $9 million over ten years. In organizing the meeting this team had gone to various civic and educational groups and asked if the groups could think of something better to do with $9 million than build a small piece of the B-1 bomber system. They invited groups to consider a fair which could be a fundraising and outreach opportunity for the organizations, a unity-builder for the neighborhood, and a chance to project a vision of how the neighborhood could be developed if it kept some of its military taxes to benefit the area.

The meeting was attended by the natural leaders of the neighborhood, both black and white, many of whom had positions in organizations. They were mostly people who cared more about their own organizations, and unity, safety, and tax resources for the neighborhood, than for international peace. One reason for coming was they liked the prospect of a team undertaking the big job of organizing a fair that would benefit their own organizations and the neighborhood.

The agenda was carefully built to give the leaders a chance to hear each other, to say how a fair could be of value, to check out the peace team's flexibility and ability to listen, and to imagine what the fair could look like. Not all the leaders knew each other, but they'd all heard of each other and needed the chance to size each other up. When the initiating team was challenged ("Are you pacifist fanatics?"), other leaders spoke up for the reasonableness of the team and pointed to the self-interest of the leaders. The meeting included small randomized groups for coming up with possible names for the fair. The winning suggestion was Fair Shake Festival, because "our neighborhood deserves a fair shake." (We immediately decided to sell milkshakes for a fundraiser!) The meeting concluded with solid enthusiasm and the fair, held six months later, was a resounding success for everyone.

—the director of the peace campaign which included the neighborhood team items first may be just right. If members are concerned about a hot topic, you may need to deal with that early in order to clear the air for other business. An item which needs attention but which can bog people down should go into a high energy slot—perhaps just after the break, or, in some groups, near the beginning.

A meeting's tone is often set right at the beginning. For that reason, some groups begin with a song, with a report of a recent victory, or with silence, chanting, or prayers. Not only do such beginnings help to create a positive tone, but they also draw the members into the "here and now" of the meeting, leaving behind the worries and preoccupations they may have brought with them.

When you are designing the meeting, notice that each agenda item is a kind of mini meeting, which has a particular outcome and a process for involving those in the meeting. Each item is a particular event with a time limit. Each can be designed differently, on the basis of time, personnel, and the needs of the group. Even though it occurs in the context of the meeting, each item has a life of its own, with a beginning, middle, and end. Each item has tasks for particular team members, and a goal to achieve. When you think of it this way, you have a key to designing high-energy meetings that bring people back for more.

> Our group likes to start its meetings by going around and letting everyone share something positive that's happened recently in their lives. It gets us off on the right foot. I guess it's a way of remembering that we don't just exist for the work we do together, and it certainly brings in the people who are shy and sometimes hold back from participating. For them it breaks the ice.
>
> —a member of a church governing council

Plan the agenda with awareness of time, and be creative in the ways you approach different agenda items.

Estimate the amount of time each agenda item needs, and put it on the agenda, so everyone can see. When the facilitator reviews the agenda in the beginning of the meeting, be open to changing the

121

estimates in light of feedback from attenders. Then, when the attenders agree to the revised agenda, they are agreeing to the discipline of time.

It helps, too, to have a timekeeper from the group whose job it is to announce when only five minutes or so are left in the time allotted to an agenda item. The group may want to extend the discussion of the item but there is now an awareness of time. People will more easily understand that time added to one agenda item means time subtracted from another—unless, of course, the group wants to extend the time of the meeting.

When ten people consider an agenda that has not been planned with an awareness of time, we can predict two to four strong personalities will dominate the discussion and argue ad nauseam. Without clear boundaries placed on time, such arguments can be both ineffective and destructive to the morale of the group. An alternative scenario among many possibilities is to ask each individual to make a two-minute presentation of her or his point of view, after taking five minutes to prepare. At the end of each two minutes, a signal warns the individual that ten seconds remain. A recorder writes the major points on chart paper. By the end of half an hour, the issues would be raised and it would be clear in which direction the group was leaning. The process is interesting, stimulating, and holds people accountable for their own views. The domination of a few is replaced by the empowerment of all, even those who initially might shrug and say they don't feel strongly one way or the other.

Use different approaches for different agenda items. Starting every item with a report followed by a whole-group discussion is like crew members not being allowed to change position in the raft and always having to paddle from the same side.

To generate new ideas or to get more options, use brainstorming. To find out quickly where people are leaning at the moment, use a straw poll. To get more energy, ask everyone to sit in a different seat. (We know it's hard to believe, but this actually works.) To shift gears after a hot debate, take a moment of quiet together. To get everyone involved, create buzz groups, where people turn to each other in threes or fours and share opinions with each other for five minutes or so.

In our experience, groups work more productively and feel better if part of their meeting is spent in subgroups. That's because more people can talk in less time in small groups. Don't be mechanical with this; not all tasks are best done in small groups. The key is to decide which tasks are appropriate for small group work and which require the whole group. Don't be surprised if the meeting resists forming small groups and then, once people are in them, they don't want to stop their animated discussions.

Include next steps and follow-up.

You'll add to the sense of accomplishment in your meeting if you consider next steps near the end of your agenda, even if you only summarize tasks which have been identified along the way. Be sure to clarify who is responsible for each next step. The group also needs to know who is going to keep track of whether the work is getting done before the next meeting. As in other areas of organizing, success builds on success. Successfully carrying out tasks between meetings results in more dynamic meetings.

Paying Attention to Process

Set up a division of labor for more effective meetings.

Create as many specialized roles as are useful. Look for ways to use everyone's skills by assigning them a role where they can succeed. Consider training all interested members in the skills they need.

One useful division of labor is to separate the roles of president and meeting facilitator. The president (chair, coordinator, or some other title) is elected to give leadership to the mission of the organization. Often she or he is a spokesperson to the media, represents the group at coalition meetings, etc. Usually the president represents the political perspective of the majority of the members, and is expected to push that perspective.

The meeting facilitator, on the other hand, takes responsibility for the conduct of the internal meetings of the organization. He or she is elected or appointed because of facilitation skills, not for a political perspective. Facilitators need to remain impartial during the meeting, although no doubt having opinions at other times. Like the name implies, a facilitator "makes easier" the work of the group, by calling on people, setting up the activities of the agenda (brainstorming, small groups, etc.), calling the vote or trying out a sense of the meeting (if consensus is used for decision-making).[2]

Another role is timekeeper, someone who keeps track of the time and lets the group know when the allotted time is half gone, nearly all used up, and gone. As described above, the group (assisted by the facilitator) can change its mind about time allocation, but it is usually easier for the facilitator and the group if someone is specifically appointed to keep an awareness of time boundaries.

Still another valuable role is process observer, sometimes called "vibes watcher." The process observer reflects back to the group how it is working: Are men chronically interrupting women? Have people seemed to stop listening to each other? Are only a few people doing all the talking? This role can make a world of difference for a group, if it is well defined and accepted by the group. How and when it is legitimate for the individual to report her or his observations must be clear. The individual in the role needs a basic understanding of both group process and of running effective meetings.

When our group experimented with having a process observer we found it was a good spot for developing courage! In the very first meeting the observer noticed a couple of patterns that some men were showing. One was that a woman would give an opinion that was ignored and a little later a man would give the same opinion and get support and a 'go-ahead' for it. Another was that several of the men talked in capital letters—no tone of suggestion or thinking out loud, but instead a tone of great authority and finality, whether they'd thought about something for years or it was completely off the top of their head. So the observer named these patterns and got resistance, big-time. We didn't resolve it at all that night and people left the meeting feeling irritated and unsettled.

But then the next week something amazing happened. One of the men said he'd been thinking about what happened, and realized he had a lot to learn, and asked for there to be a process observer! The other men didn't fight it, so we've had one for a year now and the men—and the meetings— are a thousand percent better than they used to be.

—a participant in the organization

If there is a rotating agenda committee, try appointing one of its members as the process observer, since they understand the nature of the agenda, the goals, and the background of those present. Notice that the process observer has a dual responsibility. One is to participate fully along with other members of the group. The other is to observe how the meeting is progressing and to point out when it is lost in tangents or unduly affected by insensitive or outrageous behaviors.[3]

Anticipate emotional dynamics which may bog the meeting down.

Keep in mind the hidden agenda of unfinished business that people may bring to the meeting. For example, strong leftover feelings from a previous meeting need to be explored and cleared up or they will distort the work of this meeting.

Develop some ways of dealing with the blockers: the naysayer, the bully, the intimidator, and the individual who talks the group to death. In the authors' experience, most people are ultimately predictable: blockers tend to block in the same way time after time, bullies tend to bully in the same way, and those who withdraw and won't take risks are predictable in their behavior. Because of this, if you take the time to design group meetings, you can devise ways of controlling the belligerent, antagonistic, or verbally controlling individual. Here are some specific techniques.

One way to control such an individual is to place him or her in a group of six who speak on the issue while the group listens. The ground rules include a specific amount of time for each individual, with no interruptions allowed. After the fish bowl members speak, then others in the room have their chance.

Another tactic is to structure small group work so the most verbal members are placed together. The other groups of three or four people allow plenty of opportunity for less vocal people to generate ideas and have their views considered. Or, let small groups be random and very small—two or three people. With so few people in the group, controlling behavior becomes much more apparent than in a larger group, where people are used to a few people taking the spotlight. Still another tactic, useful when you need the whole group together, is to hand out the same number of chips, matches, or small tokens to each person, and ask that each person hand in a chip each time he or she speaks. When the chips are exhausted, so is the speaking time. If your members are willing to experiment with this method, they will probably find that not only their behavior changes (with richer and more varied input as a result), but also their awareness of participation dynamics grows.

Once those who are designing a meeting begin to think strategically, ideas for minimizing obstructive behavior come easily. When you do not put time into designing, then the old destructive patterns emerge.[4]

One national organization which strongly valued equality and the empowerment of all its members tackled the blocking issue in a very upfront way. In the beginning of each session of national meetings, people chose a support person or "buddy" to sit beside. At the top of the agenda for the session was "buddy time" in which each individual would tell her or his neighbor what kind of support for participation s/he needed. "This is my first national meeting and I am shy, so I need encouragement to speak up," one person might say. "I feel very strongly about this afternoon's agenda items and need encouragement not to talk too much," another might say. The organization found that morale increased at meetings because each individual had a support system and the overall meeting was more effective in getting the wisdom of its members.

—a participant in the organization

Evaluate Your Meetings, Briefly and Well

Socrates is reported to have said that the unexamined life is not worth living. We wouldn't go quite that far about meetings. An unevaluated meeting can be worth having; but your organization will improve its use of meetings and shorten meeting time if you regularly evaluate.

The first kind of evaluation is called an interval evaluation. You establish, at the beginning, points in time when the meeting is stopped and everyone takes a look at how successfully you are meeting your goals and how well you are working together. With practice, this can take five minutes, with people talking openly about the effectiveness of the design and the kinds of interaction occurring. At that point you can make adjustments and continue the meeting. If your members are shy about saying what they think is going on, more structure can help: ask people for the two things they would do to improve the meeting, and record their suggestions on chart paper.

In a day-long meeting, try three interval evaluations spread through the day. In a three-hour meeting, try one in the middle. The point is, by setting up an expectation that evaluation is going to happen, the group is more likely to monitor itself. If your group is fairly undisciplined, try scheduling a break right after the evaluation, which reduces the chance that people will go overtime during the evaluation. The agenda committee (including the facilitator and process observer) may want to meet during the break and make adjustments in light of the evaluation.

Evaluate briefly at the end of the meeting. Sometimes meetings do end with a sense of incompleteness and tension, with some issues among the participants not resolved. At the end of a three-hour meeting, at least fifteen minutes should be set aside for a well-designed evaluation, in which people can talk about their responses to the meeting in an honest and structured manner.

Many groups do their evaluation in a brainstorm style, in which individuals make their statements without an effort to get others to agree. This is a fast way to get a lot of information, and the sensitive facilitator will notice which comments get a lot of nods of agreement. A wall chart is used, and the facilitator first asks for positives, on the rationale that a group will more likely repeat things it does well if it affirms them. The facilitator then asks, "What can we do better next time?" Sometimes a member will say both what was negative and how that negative could be changed. The facilitator doesn't press for solutions, which can be worked on by the agenda committee for the next meeting.

If this format is producing superficial responses, there may not be enough safety in the group for honest feedback, or people may not have sufficient awareness to make process observations. In that case, try asking people to form pairs or trios to come up with three strengths in how the meeting was conducted and three areas where changes are needed. The small groups can report out, with the facilitator recording on the wall chart.

On an emotional level, the evaluation at the end of the meeting can involve healing. Activists get plenty of bruises and scars from working in our society; within our organizations we want some healing to take place. Often a simple statement will be sufficient for raising awareness, for example, the evaluation of a shy person whose one contribution to the meeting had been interrupted. Other observations might be made, however, which need work outside the meeting. Two people at loggerheads might need the assistance of a third person to learn to live with their differences. You can see how the ongoing health of the organization will benefit from brief, thoughtful, and honest evaluations.

The journey we take in our organizations is marked by gathering points called meetings, which can be tedious chores or times of renewed purpose and inspiration. Groups that make use of the wisdom found in books, manuals, and workshops will find ways of continually improving their meeting life together, thereby increasing the chances of achieving their goals.

Notes

1. Helpful suggestions on this and other dimensions of meeting process can be found in Berit M. Lakey, *Meeting Facilitation: The No Magic Method* (Philadelphia and Gabriola Island, B.C.: New Society Publishers); Coover, et al, *Resource Manual for a Living Revolution; A Manual for Group Facilitators* and *Building United Judgment: A Handbook for Consensus Decision Making*, both by the Center for Conflict Resolution in Madison, WI and distributed by New Society Publishers, and *Democracy in Small Groups: Participation, Decision Making and Communication* by John Gastil, (Philadelphia and Gabriola Island, B.C.: New Society Publishers, 1993).
2. Katrina Shields clarifies the role of a meeting facilitator, and lists the qualities of good facilitation, in her manual *In the Tiger's Mouth: An Empowerment Guide for Social Action*, (Philadelphia and Gabriola Island, B.C.: New Society Publishers, 1994) pp. 94–98.
3. Process observers can benefit from the stimulating description of group dynamics in Starhawk, *Dreaming the Dark: Magic, Sex and Politics* (Boston: Beacon Press, 1982) chapter 7. A useful list of things to watch for is in Katrina Shields, *In the Tiger's Mouth*, pp. 80–82.
4. There is another level of analysis of blocking behaviors that can lead to new understanding of the group and the discovery of hidden potential. Group psychologist Arnold Mindell describes this approach in his book *The Leader as Martial Artist: Techniques and Strategies for Resolving Conflict and Creating Community* (San Francisco: HarperSanFrancisco, 1992).

Chapter 10

PADDLING AT OUR BEST

Supervising Staff and Volunteers

W E DO OUR BEST WHEN OUR VICTORIES AND EXTRA EFFORTS GET NOTICED and our weaknesses get corrective assistance; our strengths get stronger. This is true in rafting a river and even more true in working for social change. Effective organizations make sure everyone gets thought about. Volunteers, director, staff, and board members benefit from thoughtful supervision. We offer some suggestions in this chapter.

Make the Supervision Process Consistent with the Values of the Organization

The real thrust of supervision is helping people grow and become more effective in their role: it is about empowerment. The trouble is, the work ethic in our culture values doing, rather than nurturing. It is easier to evaluate and reward an effective doer who accomplishes measurable goals than it is to reward a supervisor whose job it is to help others accomplish their goals. The authors find the average supervisor says twenty-five percent of his or her time is spent supervising; seventy-five percent of his or her time is spent doing other things for which they are rewarded. If that report were accurate, fifty to seventy-five days per year would be devoted to supervisory activities—four to five hundred hours a year. The supervisors we've interviewed, offered that bit of math, usually revise their supervisory estimate downward.

> *The large action organization was suffering from low morale and high turnover. Some staff members bragged to each other about the "shit-fights" they engaged in with political or regional rivals inside the organization. Others complained constantly that the group failed internally to live up to its public statements about cooperation and a new way of life.*
>
> *The consultant brought in noticed early that managers and task leaders had little experience and no training in the art of supervision. Because the culture of the group was antiauthority, managers thought it best to hire good people and "let them go for it." In interviews with staff, however, the consultant found strong feelings of anxiety and insecurity; the projects were often high risk, the political environment outside the organization constantly shifting, and the organization's own strategy was frequently adjusted to cope with the environment. These highly motivated staff members' insecurity meant that they especially needed thoughtful supervision: someone to assure them that they were on course and assist them when they were off. Lacking reassurance, it was natural for the anxiety to be expressed in rumor-mongering, cliques, divisiveness, and a sense that "I'd better watch my back."*
>
> —from the consultant who was involved

Nonprofit groups have an advantage over businesses when it comes to supervision and the mission of the organization. While the bottom line of a business is profit, the bottom line of a social change organization is the empowerment of people. We can use our values to support an organizational culture which places supervision in a different context. Instead of providing referees for the competition over status and salary, supervision in our organizations can provide coaching and support for the growth and development of people.* Supervision does not require a traditional pyramidal structure. A collective can create a framework for supervision by asking who will be most helpful in supervising whom. The point is to make sure that

---

* One of the authors, Rod Napier, has found in his practice that salary is a relatively poor motivating factor for productivity, even in corporate life. Those who are passed over for salary increments usually feel resentful and become either passive or belligerent. Those who receive a salary increment feel appreciative in the short run and then typically change their attitude and decide that they deserved it all along and feel no reason to make any extra effort.

everyone in the group gets the quality attention she or he deserves.

Increasing effectiveness is what supervision is about. It is a myth that supervision is needed to prod people into action, into working harder. The reality is that a highly motivated person may be ineffective in getting her or his job done well. Usually, working smarter is more important than working harder. Even when a group understands that supervision supports empowerment, some members are likely to mistrust it. Activists who have chosen to work outside the mainstream in order to maintain some sense of their own freedom and integrity may worry about unnecessary control, constraints to personal freedom, and narrowly based judgements. Nearly all of us have some personal experience with arbitrary and subjective evaluations, which often began with grading in school.

Despite the frequency of negative past experiences, the authors have found that people in organizations are extraordinarily open to being helped and to learning, as long as they do not feel stupid or punished. The secret is creating a context for personal development within the organization, so feedback and review are a natural part of any process and do not occur only when something is wrong.

Treat Ongoing Volunteers as Unpaid Staff

In too many organizations volunteers are an afterthought, doing what the staff doesn't want to do, expected to be here today and gone tomorrow. Volunteers can actually be critical to the success of the organization, providing needed skills and energy.

We needed an initial staff of at least six even to have a chance to win a referendum in our city, but we had money only for one and a half! We decided to pay an overall coordinator and a training/volunteer coordinator, and recruit volunteers to do the rest. We created job descriptions, interviewed people who were interested, and appointed two field organizers, an office manager, and a policy staff person—all of them unpaid. They worked two to four days per week, depending on their other jobs and circumstances. Our volunteer coordinator/trainer was careful in interviewing to make sure volunteers were clear about what they could get out of these positions—how their own goals could be advanced.

As the campaign grew we were able to hire some additional organizers and a full time office secretary, but we kept the unpaid staff—we needed them, and they found their work satisfying. These core volunteers (there were a lot of other volunteers who gave less time) were treated like staff in every way: staff meetings, supervision, staff development opportunities like workshops and conferences, status, supervisory roles regarding other volunteers. The only difference from paid staff was that they were not paid.

It was easier in the heat of a referendum to get volunteers to commit large amounts of time to the campaign, but even after we won, a tradition of unpaid staff continued for years. There was some turnover, but some paid staff turned over, too. The main thing was that the campaign received a lot of top-quality, highly responsible work from this dedicated group.

—former coordinator of the organization, which was a coalition of justice and peace groups in a large east coast city

Even though today's economy of two-job families makes recruitment of volunteers a challenge, volunteers exist. Look for students, people who are between jobs, people who are returning to the job market and need to build their resumes and learn new skills, newcomers to the community interested in plugging in, and retired people who can now devote their skills and time to their interests. Define your target group in order to focus your appeal to them. Advertising is one way to recruit: community newspapers, bulletin boards at colleges and universities, local churches, volunteer fairs, volunteer clearing houses, computer bulletin boards, and public service announcements on radio and television. The most productive means of recruitment of volunteers, however, is through existing members and volunteers—over seventy percent are recruited this way.

Treating volunteers as staff clarifies the relationship enormously. Most of the advice in this chapter applies to volunteers as well as paid staff. "You can't fire a volunteer!" is a myth; like paid staff, volunteers sometimes need to be let go.

Create a System of Supervison

Overseeing the work of others, or accountability, is at the heart of supervision, but it entails several parts. To get a job done, there must be a definition of the job, a gathering of needed resources, a clarification of the level of authority that goes with the job, a picture of

132

> *One of our newer volunteers brought useful skills and considerable charm—he was a real people person. In fact, he spent more and more time socializing with other members and started missing deadlines. After a couple of meetings with his supervisor, it became clear that his passion was really more for partying than for the cause, and he halfway acknowledged it himself. We fired him, and the morale in the organization rose immediately. I was surprised by how much his failure to come through at a high level of excellence was disturbing the others in the group.*

—executive director of a peace group

how the job fits into the larger scheme of things, and regular meetings with someone for sharing information, coaching, and feedback.

Design the job carefully and describe it clearly, whether to be carried out by a paid staff member or a volunteer. Time is wasted and confusion occurs when people are asked to carry out an ill-defined job. Whether you are recruiting a new person or reassigning someone to carry out a new project, write a job description:

- tasks to be done
- expectations of performance
- kind of experience being sought or training available to make up gaps in experience and skills
- timeframe (permanent/temporary, full-time/part-time, etc.)
- level of authority for making decisions
- who will supervise

If a person is to be held responsible for a job they must have the authority to make decisions. Too often, people are asked to take responsibility for a job but denied commensurate authority to get the job done. They are left frustrated and set up to take blame for things gone wrong even though not receiving credit when things go well. Some supervisors think they must be the experts in a given area, and thus exert too much control by withholding authority. In fact, their responsibility is to select the best person to get the job done, provide the freedom they need to work, and provide assistance as they request.

Provide Access to Resources

"Resources" may be facilities, materials, organizing contacts, leads to volunteers, access to the public relations unit in the organization, and the like. Volunteers and staff members find it extremely frustrating to be ready to work but to lack the resources. Some organizations fill up their supervisors' workload with tasks that leave them little time for actual supervision, resulting in bottlenecks and wasted time for staff members and volunteers who are waiting for the resources they need.

How a project or position fits into the whole organization is crucial for success. Often in social change organizations the structure is loose, in the name of operating a democratic organization or out of fear of appearing hierarchical. The looseness may appear to be more comfortable, but actually increases confusion, anxiety, and even hostility when one part of the organization clashes with another. When a person is asked to work without a clear idea of how what they do fits into the organization's strategy and structure, that person is being asked to work in the dark. Working in the dark makes it hard to see the boundaries, to maintain clear communication links, or to maintain the authority that goes with the job. This is also true when the person responsible for supervision is not clearly designated, or when supervision is divided.

Orient Carefully

Orientation needs to include not only the requirements of the position or project, but also the criteria for success. The orientation provides the first description of how the job fits into organizational mission and goals. Training and staff or volunteer development is most easily put on the agenda at that first meeting. An agreement is made on frequency of supervisory meetings.

The most important aim of the orientation is to create an open channel between supervisor and volunteer or staff member, so that hesitations and questions can be raised by the staff member as they come up. The chief block to accomplishing this aim is the widespread fear of being supervised. Bruising earlier encounters with teachers, then bosses, have resulted in fears that usually can't be swept aside by rhetoric. The staff member or volunteer will need to see that the supervisor actually walks his or her talk.

During the days of the "War on Poverty" programs, the federal government made grants to traditional institutions for various community programs. There were community advisory boards put in place to advise the institutions regarding the community's needs. There was an individual hired as an executive director by the institution and the community together. The executive director was paid by the institution (from the grant) and was responsible to the institution and to the community advisory board. The executive director was accountable to each of these entities and often found her/himself caught in the middle in any crossfire. There was a large turnover in executive directors, where this confusion was cited as a major cause. One executive director put it this way: "I knew that unless I got them to talk with each other before they came to me on a policy directive, I would lose my mind and the organization would be unable to do the job it was set up to do. So, I accepted the job with the clear stipulation that the director of the institution would meet with the chairperson of the community advisory board and myself on a regular basis, if I were to take the job."

—a former executive director in a community health center in New York City

Develop Mutual Relationships

The best supervisory process is one in which individuals believe that it is in their best interest and that of the organization to develop each person as fully as possible. If they believe a supervisor truly is interested in their growth and will help them, then they will come to trust the supervisory process. However, personal growth and development, by its very nature, assumes the involvement of individuals themselves along with their supervisor. This means supervision becomes even more threatening, potentially, and the individual even more exposed as personal limitations and strengths are explored in the context of the job.

The best way to minimize this naturally threatening situation is to have the supervisor model vulnerability. The supervisor persuades the staff person that the supervisor needs information about his or her own performance in order to grow personally and develop professionally. If the supervisor is seen to be open to such feedback and to respond to it in a direct and meaningful way, it will be easier for the person supervised to do the same.

Creating a feedback system for people you supervise has two

advantages: providing credibility and helping you to improve your work. Both the credibility and the personal improvement will further enhance your ability to assist those you supervise to do their very best. Here is a survey instrument which you can use to get feedback. You may want to fill it out yourself as well, in order to understand it better and to improve the supervision you receive.

Effective Supervision Survey

Use this instrument to assess the behavior of your supervisor. Be honest.

Your responses will be anonymous and help your supervisor determine behaviors which are effective and those which need strengthening.

To the left of each item rate your supervisor on a scale of 1–10 (10 = excellent), and to the right rate the degree (1–10) to which you would like to receive this kind of attention.

The supervisor:
- Clearly defines her or his own limit of authority.
- Provides me with a clear understanding of my own authority as it relates to my role.
- Provides me and others with clear organizational goals and priorities.
- Helps me to establish my own goals and objectives in an atmosphere of openness and collaboration, where my ideas and concerns are seriously considered.
- Determines with me the criteria of success upon which my own performance will be measured.
- Believes that my career development is a crucial part of the supervisory process and actively focuses with me on career opportunities and my own long term goals.
- Meets with me regularly to keep in touch with my progress and explore my concerns.
- Establishes with me a climate of help and accessibility that makes it easy to approach him or her.
- Provides me with organizational information I feel is important to my own work and maintains my interest and involvement in the organization.

- Provides me with the opportunity to develop specific skills or experience necessary for my present job or future development within this organization or elsewhere.
- Helps me develop a clear and easily followed plan that outlines my progress and how well I am meeting my own goals and objectives, both in terms of the job itself and my person and professional development.
- Helps me evaluate my own performance in areas of strengths and limitations.
- Takes time periodically to observe me on the job, doing those things that are most important for my success.
- Solicits my own views of my performance based on the criteria to which we previously agreed.
- Solicits, along with me, information from individuals I impact in my job and compares this with his or her conceptions of my performance, as well as with my own.
- Works with me to improve my performance in areas that appear to need strengthening, based on the information I have gathered.
- Gives problems I have within the organization appropriate attention, shortly after I've stated them.
- Involves me in problem solving where I have the expertise or where I feel the eventual decision will directly influence my own life.

An additional way to develop supervisor credibility is to share with those you supervise the organizational goals, where you and your staff and volunteers fit in, and your individual goals for the coming year and how you will be measured and held accountable for them. The more a supervisor can establish his or her own goals, specific objectives, and measures of success, and the more willing she or he is to share these, the more those supervised will be eager to do the same.

Suit the Supervision to the Person

Not everyone requires the same kind of supervision. A newcomer to a job deserves and expects a more intense level of supervision as she or he becomes familiar with the work, establishes goals, and builds the support systems needed for success. Some individuals are already familiar with the work, achievement oriented, and skillful to such a degree that work gets done on time with excellence; they need much less time. Be cautious however: people who are skilled often find it difficult to ask for help. Supervisors need to stay close enough to keep the lines open for tactful intervention.*

Stay Resourceful by Staying in Touch with New Developments in Your Field

Your supervision is stronger if you are staying informed of changes, learning new skills and perspectives, and learning how to pass them on to those you supervise. Reading the latest articles and networking with counterparts in other organizations working on the same issues keep you fresh and maximally helpful.

Make Evaluation a Fully Participative, and Positive, Process

For social change organizations, the aim of a successful evaluation is greater empowerment for achieving goals and correcting weaknesses. This can most easily be done with a positive tone and maximum interaction.

One way to create a positive and participative evaluation session is to hold a brief meeting three days to a week ahead of time to outline the format and expectations and to answer questions. While a certain amount of anxiety is a natural part of any major evaluation or performance review, the meeting can also be perceived as a real opportunity for planning, development, and learning. The supervisor should quickly review his or her own goals and how the individual fits into the supervisor's area of accountability. It is also useful to review the givens, the nonnegotiable expectations that are established by the supervisor and need to be accepted by the supervisee as part of the framework of the job and the organization. This discussion lays important groundwork for the later one.

At this point a series of questions are given to be used to prepare for the evaluation. Each question is answered twice by the supervisee:

---

* Such an intervention requires a sensitive judgement call. We are clearly not advocating a second-guessing or meddling approach, which is sometimes justified with the concept of coaching. (See chapter 7 on the windowshade concept of authority.)

> *We were a really inexperienced bunch of rafters for taking on the Colorado, but our river guide didn't seem to mind. He complimented us on even little things we did right, until our confidence rose, and he was patient about showing us how to change the things we did wrong. Sometimes we were all talking at once in the beginning, trying to get it right before we hit the first whitewater. Even though I was plenty nervous, it being my first time, I still noticed how gung ho our guide was, like he believed in us even when we made mistakes.*
>
> —a long-time activist who has directed a number of nonprofits

once from his or her own perspective and once as she or he imagines the supervisor would answer it. The supervisor is responding also. Note that no set of questions will evoke an honest dialogue about performance if the relationship is marked by distrust. If the supervisory relationship has been at least adequate, however, questions like these (answered by both parties, and answered twice by the person supervised) will stimulate a high degree of honesty and nondefensiveness and prepare the way for improved performance in the future:

1. Please note three to five of your greatest successes or achievements on the job during the past six months or year. What led you to pick those?
2. What do you like most about working in this organization?
3. What kinds of things do you like least about working here?
4. Please note three to five things you would have liked to have accomplished over the course of the last year but didn't.
5. What do you see as your most important areas of responsibility during the coming year? Explain clearly the projects, goals, and outcomes you wish to achieve. What kind of time will each of these projects or specific goals require from you?
6. What measures would you establish to determine if you have been successful or not in completing your goals and projects? Please be as specific as possible.
7. What factors, either personal, supervisory, or organizational, might block you from being effective in accomplishing these particular goals?

8. What responses, skills, education, experiences, or special help do you think you will need to accomplish these goals in the most successful way possible?

In the evaluation session itself, the supervisor's first aim is to evoke a maximum of information and acknowledgement of how things have gone. The set of questions is a tool for that. Each question can lead to interesting discussion and new information, if the style is conversational exploration rather than interview. The supervisor needs to probe, inquire, and encourage a convergence of perspectives on the staff member's or volunteer's performance.* If an important discrepancy is discovered between the views of the two, the discussion can move deeper. Disagreements can lead to valuable new understandings: for example, of differences rooted in culture, or of uncommunicated organizational constraints and traditions.

The second aim is to negotiate changes. We use the term "negotiate" in order to acknowledge that, even in grassroots and nonprofit organizations, staff members' interests may differ somewhat from the organization's. Even when there is full agreement on the givens, which were reiterated in the preparatory meeting, there is usually a great deal of room within which the staff member can maneuver, in terms of how the job gets done and how ill-defined quantities of time are actually spent. Ideally, the organization receives what it needs and wants from individuals. But an employee's or volunteer's needs for training, new experiences, and certain responsibilities may be at odds with the organizational interests and needs at any particular point in time.

Since satisfied workers produce more, have less down time and absenteeism, and win more allies for the organization, it only makes sense that the closer one can come to meeting both organizational and individual needs, the better off one will be. The negotiation, therefore, is to maximize the benefit to both staff member or volunteer and organization. A question about goals and timelines leads naturally to this dialogue. There is no use in entrapping anyone into commitments they will not be able to keep. The goal of the supervisor is the success of the staff member. It is her or his job to help the individual clarify

* See chapter 13 for advice on how to give feedback in ways which will reduce defensiveness.

what needs to be done and why and to make sure the goals of the individual also reflect the needs of the organization. Underlying this are three principles:

- If you want to be successful, you first have to know what will constitute success.
- The more precisely success is defined, the easier it will be to decide the best way to get there.
- If the path to success is precisely marked and laid out, it will be easier to keep track of how things are going along the way.

The negotiation opens the door to help an individual know what is to be achieved, to be aware of how much freedom he or she has while achieving the goals, and to know how well she or he is progressing toward the goals. There is plenty of room to take into account the specific nature of the job, which might be unique, the experience and qualifications of of the individual, and the kind of supervision which is appropriate given these realities. This is a natural point for the supervisee to press for changes in the kind of supervision she or he feels is needed. The wise supervisor knows that the person wearing the shoe knows best where it pinches.

Underlying all of this is the strong belief that as individuals help to develop specific goals and targets for performance, they experience more internal control and success: empowerment.

Put Supervision in Context

Create a contract to support the relationship. A contract in a supervisory relationship may seem needlessly formal, but we recommend it in order not to leave the results of negotiation to memory and possibly demoralizing confusion. A contract simply details what has been agreed to for the coming year: key job responsibilities, expected results, how results will be measured and what kind of supervision. The contract can be useful in avoiding misunderstandings, increasing accountability, and providing opportunities along the way for midcourse correction.

Some supervisory relationships start out strong, then deteriorate in the crush of work, sometimes leaving staff members out of touch when they need a supervisor most. Because jobs and individuals differ, a rule about frequency of supervision meetings is not useful. Connecting frequency of supervision specifically to the work plan and contract is a way of individualizing the process while holding both parties accountable for seeing that staff and volunteers get the attention they deserve.

Part of the role of the supervisor is to develop an informal and trusting relationship with the supervisee that includes, but also goes beyond, the structured contract. A cool, impersonal attitude is not realistic or necessary in this process. There are no pat formulas for developing a warmer kind of relationship. Informally dropping in on the volunteer or staff person, occasionally going to lunch, and being aware of what is important in other aspects of his or her life can go a long way in breaking down barriers and developing a constructive climate for work. This does not necessitate being friends or buddies with those you supervise; think of the golden rule: supervise as you would like to be supervised. Build a relationship with open and honest communication, based on a range of experiences; this provides the means through which you can become an ally for the empowerment of those you supervise.

In our experience, organizational cultures typically resist effective supervision: supervisors are overloaded with other work to do, feel less competent than others, want to avoid seeming to be authoritarian, worry about how accountability relates to diversity issues in the organization, or all of the above. This means that leadership needs to face resistance and overcome it in order to allow supervision to reach its potential.

Unless your organization is quite exceptional, you will need to create consequences and rewards to encourage effective supervision. Accountability needs to come to the seat of authority in your group, whatever its internal structure: leadership needs to demonstrate that failure to supervise effectively results in loss of leadership position.

There are specific behavioral measures that can be used. Insist that the eight-question evaluation interview described above happen once each year, with a report prepared by the supervisor. The eight-question format is, in our experience, highly effective if used fully; it provides the opportunity for supervisors to motivate, to explain, to demonstrate, and, through active listening, to assist with problem solving. Another measure is to have supervisees evaluate the

> The scientists in a major university who were managing important research projects needed to learn to be more effective supervisors in order to produce quality work. The consultants who were brought in to lead a supervision skills workshop noted that the scientists tended to have a tone of antibureaucracy and antiauthority which usually goes with resistance to becoming effective supervisors; nevertheless, by the end of the workshop the scientists became enthusiastic about making changes in their practice.
>
> Two years later the lead consultant was telephoned by a top research manager who was extremely frustrated because the scientists did not follow through. They all expressed enthusiasm for what they learned, but they failed to implement it.
>
> —the lead consultant in the project

supervisors; earlier in this chapter we offered a format for that. A third measure is through work plans. Our experience is that when we ask supervisors how much time should be given to supervision, a typical response is fifty percent. When we ask how much they actually do, they typically say twenty-five percent. When we then ask whether they spend more than one full day a week, they typically acknowledge that they spend much less time than that. Since time reflects priority and value, leaders can use work plans to emphasize that doing the work of supervising takes time and needs time.

Chapter 11

BUILDING HIGH MORALE

How to Develop and Maintain the Spirit of the Crew

WHEN YOUR ORGANIZATION IS RUSHING THROUGH WHITE WATER—OR even when it is in a slow moving current—the attitude of the members and staff is critical to success. Morale is to the group what self-esteem is to the individual: it is the sense of value and pride a group has in itself. The condition of a group's sense of well-being may seem mysterious, but there are actually a number of specific things you can do to improve morale, even in a group that has a history of despair.

Boost Morale by Paying Attention to It

Organizational leaders sometimes act as if high morale comes automatically with the righteousness of the cause. We've seen too many demoralized groups working for great causes to believe there is anything automatic about morale.

How much attention morale needs depends on the group's mission. If you are operating in a high stress environment or expect many long and arduous campaigns before achieving your goals, you will need to give major attention to morale. This requires thoughtful understanding of some of the antimorale demons which harass organizations for social change: media fixation, shutting down after losing a battle, righteous judgmentalism, internalized oppression, and the split between the personal and the political.

Don't Believe the Media

A contradiction in many social change activists is the belief, on the one hand, that the major media organizations are owned by corporations and protect the status quo, and on the other hand, that we can safely believe what the media report about how social change is (or is not) progressing. If the media are indeed biased against social movements, why do we frequently look to them to validate our work?

The authors suggest that this tendency is the natural consequence of all those thousands of hours many of us spend watching, listening, and reading the mass media. To escape such conditioning would be a miracle. Further complicating the picture is that media coverage sometimes has played a part in movement victories, for example in the civil rights movement. When positive coverage occurs, we may falsely generalize and imagine that the media are basically neutral and objective.

This does not mean we should stop reading the newspapers and watching television. It does mean that we need our own sources of information, magazines and newsletters that highlight and explore stories that are buried in the mainstream media.[1] We also need our own framework of interpretation to understand the significance of the reports. One reason we started this book with Bill Moyer's model of social change movements is that it gives us a far more useful way of interpreting events than that of the media.

For example, throughout the 1970s and 1980s, journalists routinely described demonstrations as "reminiscent of the 'sixties." The most amusing case of this was reports about the 1982 march of one million against nuclear weapons in New York City. The largest march in the 1960s was in 1963 at the Lincoln Memorial in Washington, with 250,000. Predictably, journalists said that the million-strong march in New York was "reminiscent of the 'sixties." That kind of media spin is irritating, especially if we are expecting fair coverage. Another way of interpreting that coverage is as evidence of how scared the powerholders were of what happened in the 1960s in the United States, and how eager they were not to encourage any more of it. With each viewing of media coverage which minimizes and discounts our work, we can in fact draw support for how powerful social movements can be.

This is not to say that mass media never report fairly on our efforts;

145

they do sometimes. Furthermore, activists have a responsibility to reach out to journalists to increase the fairness of coverage; there are materials and workshops available which boost the chances of fair coverage of our efforts.[2] The trick is for us to stay balanced: to relate to the media enthusiastically, while keeping a realistic picture. Organizational leaders need to maintain this balanced perspective in order not to get trapped by media-related mood swings.

It is not only unfair media coverage which drags down morale, but also the content of what is reported. Powerholders are fairly consistent in their wish not to affirm the power of social movements, and they use the media for that purpose. The media announced President Richard Nixon's intention to watch the football game instead of the giant antiwar march in November, 1969; Nixon's people wanted activists to get the message that their action was less important than sports. An alternative view: Nixon was worried enough about the antiwar movement to respond by sending that message.

I remember how hard we pushed to get a ban on nuclear testing in the atmosphere. Some pacifists even sailed into the Pacific Ocean testing zone to protest, putting their own lives in danger. When John Kennedy came into the White House the movement grew, but he resisted the push. Then the Soviets unilaterally stopped testing and the U.S. public grew more insistent that the United States stop poisoning the air with radioactive dust. Finally Kennedy gave in. I was not prepared for the media's spin: the ban suddenly became 'Kennedy's treaty' and a validation of how wise and statesmanlike he was!

—a peace organizer who started his activism in the late 1950s and early 1960s

---

It can also be demoralizing to have powerholders coopt movement goals. There is a dilemma here: movement leadership does not want to postpone victory by refusing to allow powerholders to save face. The dilemma points to the need for continual education of members in the power of social movements, so they understand the nature of the process and can celebrate success and feel empowered by it, rather than see victories taken from them through the posturing of powerholders.[3]

Learn from Your Losses

Paint a picture of your group as a learning organization, eager to benefit from whatever your experiences are, both positive and negative. In carefully evaluating your apparent losses, you'll be surprised how much you've gained, as this long-time Native American activist organizing among the Lakota people points out:

> We learn from our losses. There are always things to celebrate, for example, we fought a pipeline and lost the fight. We were successful because we raised the issue so that most people had information to make choices, and they understood that they had a right to decide. To be overridden by the U.S. government helped to radicalize people who may have been more complacent. Look at what we could have done—e.g., if we had more money, we could have done more—ask, where do we get the money? Maintain integrity to the issue and politics. Defeat is easier if you maintained integrity—e.g., we made a decision not to accept money from the liquor industry.

Replace Self-righteousness with Self-respect

Political groups often increase their morale by emphasizing how right they are. This emphasis seems quite reasonable; after all, people wouldn't work for change if they didn't think their point of view was correct. For so many of us, the story of our becoming activists includes a critical moment when we realized that we were right and someone else was wrong, and that it was a matter of personal integrity that we stand up for our point of view. These stories deserve to be told and these moments celebrated.

> I love to go to demonstrations or conferences which are in another city or town and drive there with a few other people. It's a great chance to get to know each other better. One of the things I do is get people to tell how they became an activist. It's inspiring and we arrive at the demonstration ready to really go for it.
>
> —a New England tenant organizer

The problem is a subtle one: how to be right without being self-righteous. The difference lies in the emphasis on how wrong others are. If I find myself frequently talking about "those idiots," "those racists," "those sexists," "those wimps," I'm playing at self-righteous superiority or judgmentalism. The emphasis on others' wrongness has the effect of avoiding full responsibility for my own life.

On a group level, we are talking about the culture of the organization: is the group trying to maintain its morale by disparaging everyone else, trying to affirm the rightness of its cause by distancing itself from others? In its purest form, this is what political sects do; one reason they stay so small is that their self-righteousness gets in the way of communication.*

Of course most social change groups are not sects, but we can learn from the sectarians what to avoid. They paint their opposition in the worst possible colors, and each time morale sags they try to affirm their rightness by making everyone else even worse, even potential allies.

Not only does this approach to building morale hurt communication; it also justifies poor strategy. Strategizing for social change requires great flexibility: experimenting with new

> The telephone caller asked me to call the pastor of a church I knew and ask permission to sell pies after the service as a benefit. I politely declined. "Why not?" the caller asked. "Well," I hesitated, "it has to do with how your organization comes across, and I'm not sure you want that feedback just now." "Tell me, tell me!" the caller begged. I gave the feedback, and was immediately attacked, guilt-tripped, and called a racist.
>
> —a neighborhood organizer in a large East Coast city

approaches, staying creative, noticing what is working, and changing what is not working. Self-righteousness destroys that flexibility and justifies failed strategies. If the government is not responding to our demands, it just shows how oppressive and unjust it is (and how right we are). If allies don't come to our side to fight with us, it just shows

---

* By political sects we mean groups which have the form of religious sects except that their doctrine is about politics instead of theology: they have a tight membership structure, a strong us versus them attitude, an elaborate and detailed worldview which is held to rigidly, and often an authoritarian leader.

148

what wimps and elitists they are (and how right we are). If our membership is not growing among the desired constituency, it just shows how misled and ignorant they are (and how right we are).

Self-righteousness rigidifies our strategies and distorts communication with people outside the group. It also drags down relationships within the group, and in the longer run undermines the very morale being right is supposed to support. When our organizational culture supports the habit of feeling superior, the habit grows until it eats the work of our colleagues as well. Quality work in social change requires creativity, as we have pointed out, which requires an open atmosphere of experimentation and permission to make mistakes and be vulnerable. A culture of righteous judgmentalism is the opposite of an open atmosphere; when volunteers and staff members operate defensively, minimizing risk of overt or covert criticism, the quality of work goes down, and morale goes down.

The alternative to self-righteousness is self-respect. When we respect ourselves and our organization we do not need to put others down; we affirm our achievements, our efforts, and each other. We recognize how far we've come, and in that context we acknowledge the many mistakes we made along the way (the ways we've been sexist, racist, etc.). We applaud our courage that, knowing we'll make more mistakes in the future, we persevere. In the civil rights movement of the 1960s a modified gospel song which organizers sometimes sang together was "I'm so glad that we are in this fight." They would go around and in each verse name a different individual who was present in the circle: "I'm so glad that _____ is in this fight/ Singing Glory, Halleluja! I'm so glad." Personal storytelling, singing, and sharing the victories and the fears with good listeners are all ways of promoting self-respect in the organization.

Another means of promoting self-respect is through regular evaluations with the work team. If there is no institutional way for people to give feedback to each other, some members will dodge their own responsibility to give feedback and use their criticism as mental support for their own feelings of superiority: "I can't believe she did that; I would certainly not make such a blunder." Or, they might criticize others behind their back. One method which works well for supporting the growth of individuals and facilitating feedback is estimation/self-estimation.[4] It works like this:

149

The volunteer, board member, or staff person who is the focus of the session meets with the three to seven people in the best position to give feedback on her or his participation in the organization. The session begins with each participant sharing memories of the focus person: affirmative stories which can also be amusing. Then the focus person makes a statement, which might include personal goals in working with the group, changes that might be underway or contemplated, how she or he has seen her or himself grow since joining the group, etc. There might be questions or responses from the other participants. Then the focus person lists (preferably with a chart) positives in their performance since the last session, with illustrations. Other participants respond by emphasizing a positive, disagreeing with the focus person on a positive, or adding to the list of positives. Next the focus person lists areas where they feel they need to grow, with illustrations. Participants respond similarly: emphasizing, disagreeing, or adding to the list of growth areas. The agenda proceeds with next steps: the whole group discusses possible action steps which might be taken as a result of the session (for example, the focus person going to a training workshop to enhance a needed skill). The session ends with an evaluation of how it went and more affirmations for the focus person.

> A major national organization was bogged down with low morale, with resulting lowered productivity while the staff spent time gossiping, politicking, and complaining. Despite this, the organization was winning some important victories. An outside consultant found that few of the staff knew about the victories outside their immediate program. When asked why they didn't know of them, they claimed they didn't have time to tell each other!
>
> —*the organizational consultant*

In larger organizations, the committee doing the estimation/self-estimation needs to develop a process so people who are not on the committee but have comments or questions can raise them through committee members.

This kind of evaluation provides a humane means through which everyone—including leaders—can get the feedback they need for growth. Members get an assured opportunity to express their thoughts rather than bury them or express them through idle complaining.

Confront Internalized Oppression

Many activists now acknowledge this: the arrows of negativity that hit us often lodge deep inside. Even though we break off the part of the arrow that shows in order to look good, the hurt remains. Racist messages from society—both obvious and subtle—are often absorbed and retained, damaging the self-image of people of color. So also with classist, heterosexist, ageist, anti-Semetic, ableist, sexist, and other oppressive messages. Recently we have been uncovering an oppressive attitude toward activists as well, delivered not only through the media but also through many families ("What are you going to do when you grow up, dear?") and peer groups (How many activists skip their school reunions?)

There were a lot of messages coming through all of this that no matter what you do it isn't good enough...the earliest messages of invalidation that I received were from my family—a southern black family with short-haired dark-skinned daughters can be quite brutal. We were not the Jack and Jill stereotypes that they wanted. I always thought I was a tragedy to my mom because she had hazel eyes that were not passed on to me. I am learning to take the power out of that invalidation. There will be attempts to invalidate me but only I determine if I let them succeed. I don't know who it was, I think that it was Eleanor Roosevelt who said something about, "Nobody can be oppressed without their permission." I have stopped giving permission to be oppressed. But, I still operate out of it— I wouldn't still be smoking cigarettes if I were not still angry with myself. That is a part of being angry with yourself—not taking care of yourself.

—a leading organizer with a national African American group

If internalized oppression is not named and confronted, it will drag down the morale of the organization in several ways:

- Damaged self-respect. When people don't respect themselves, they may substitute self-righteousness, as we have described above.
- Irrational attacks on the leaders. The more oppressed a group is, the harder it is on its leaders. The reason for this is internalized oppression—people project their negativity on those most visible and their own feelings of powerlessness on those in their group acting most powerfully.
- Divisiveness in the group. This shows up as complaining rather than taking responsibility to give feedback or correct situations, making nonnegotiable demands, turning conflicts into win/lose situations, gossiping, and backbiting.
- Pessimism. Experiments won't work, bold action will backfire, social betterment is impossible anyway, and we might as well just talk about our beliefs rather than expect real change.

Internalized oppression also has a negative impact on strategy, since a chronic feeling of unworthiness can encourage people to settle for far less than is available. Throughout these last couple of decades of progress on gay civil rights, for example, many gay men have been willing to settle for some tolerance rather than insist on full equality and acceptance of sexual diversity. In the early 1990s new groups such as Queer Nation surfaced with more ambitious demands. One reason why renewed surges of activity generally come from young people may be that, having grown up in a less oppressive cultural climate, they feel less weighed down by internalized oppression and more able to be visionary.

Malcolm X took as his major life task the overcoming of internalized oppression among African Americans. Late in his life he went to Mecca as a pilgrim and found even more self-respect as part of a global religious movement which did not need to put down others in order to worship and experience worthiness. When he returned, he acknowledged his overly critical posture toward other civil rights leaders and declared his intention to work with them in the future.[5]

Knit Together the Personal and the Political

One of the hardships activists face is the split in the culture between the personal and the political. Historically this is a result of sexism: the woman's place in the white middle and upper classes was in the home, supervising the work of personal care and maintenance; the man's place was in the market and handling political affairs. Opponents to woman suffrage argued that letting women into the political arena would mean either a loss to society of nurturing qualities, or an outrageous invasion of caring and com-passion into politics, either of which would be a disaster.

Our organizations still suffer from this historic split. Women, and men, who try to tear down the wall between personal and political are contemptuously called "touchy-feely" and endanger their credibility for leadership in "the real world" of struggles for change. And so we know organizations with extensive smoking, alcohol and drug abuse, broken agreements, personal vendettas, and an angry and stressed-out staff—in short, low morale—which think their problems are political.

Much of the wall separating personal from political is composed of the martyr syndrome. The martyr regards her or himself as sacrificing for the good of the cause. The long hours of work, the neglect of relationships, the neglect of personal time, and the lack of adequate compen-sation all add up to nobility. The martyr

> The coalition had been working for economic justice for several years, and although the staff had consistently been biracial, its teamwork showed substantial communication gaps. The director arranged for the entire staff (and some board members) to go to a personal growth seminar together. The seminar did not specifically address racial issues; nevertheless, the staff came immediately to a new level of communication and cooperation.
>
> —*former executive director of the coalition*

assumes the incompatibility between personal well-being and the collective good; the harsher the choice was for the martyr to make, the more likely she or he will resent others in the organization who do not make that choice, with predictable results for morale.

Organizational leaders can challenge the martyr syndrome by breaking out of a win/lose mentality and asking how the individual's agenda dovetails with the organizational agenda. Putting this only in terms of skills is needlessly narrow. A better result is likely from considering the whole person. For example, Joe was brought up poor, and worries a lot about money. The organization where he is on the staff is coming into hard times financially. He could complain and worry all the more, or he could see that a way in which the organization is challenged dovetails with a personal challenge for him, which is linked to classist oppression. Various options are open to him at that point: a support group with others who've been brought up poor; a buddy relationship with someone from the middle or upper class who has emotional support skills; a personal growth workshop on abundance/prosperity/money; etc. By seeing himself (and others seeing him) as having a personal issue which coincides with an organizational challenge, Joe gets to turn a time of misery into a time of growth, which can pay off not only for himself but also for the organization.

"What memories do you have of lifestyle characteristics of your families when you were growing up?" The facilitators asked. "We'll list them on this chart, brainstorm fashion."

The facilitators were addressing a gathering of fifty members of an organization that decided to tackle the impact of class in order to be more effective in working for change, but wanted to avoid an external, doctrinaire approach. A list quickly emerged on the wall: summer camp, jelly glasses on the dinner table, children getting after-school jobs, European travel, socializing with relatives rather than hosting parties for friends, and so on.

The group then divided the list into lifestyle characteristics which seemed to belong together and arranged themselves in various parts of the room according to which category seemed most like their own early life experience. Within these small groups, members shared their experience of growing up in that stratum of society.

When the small groups came back together, facilitators led a discussion which linked the previous exercise to U.S. class structure. The evening was rich with personal/political insights. Some members needed to switch groups, having been told by their parents, for example, that they were

---

middle class, whereas in fact they were working class or even poor. Some members "came out" as rich people for the first time. Some members had been in families that had changed class positions, and began to understand their own uneasiness or sense of isolation that they carried even as adults.

The facilitators closed with a challenge to continue the work of understanding class through the "identity groups" formed that evening and keep the facilitators informed so next steps could be developed for the organization. The process touched off an intense period of confrontation, self-discovery, and organizational innovation. The working class identity group became an ongoing caucus which monitored the organization's publications and practices for classism; the group also held a dramatic "speak-out" in which its members stood before the organization and told with honesty and emotion what it is like to experience class domination in both the society at large and within the organization. Upper middle class members also met for support as they tackled the guilt associated with privilege; they encouraged each others' thoughtful decisions on how to use their resources to benefit the movement for change.

Morale Reflects Many Aspects of the Organization—and Also the Intention of the Individual

The good news about organizational development is that making needed changes in the organization will improve morale, which in turn will improve the chances of achieving your social change goals. Clarifying the relation between the board and the staff, creating new norms and methods for conflict resolution, improving supervision, and facilitating better meetings—not to mention dances, potlucks, and parties—all these and more will enhance morale.

But what of the readers of this book who at this point feel like the boy who noticed the emperor wasn't wearing any clothes? You may feel alone in seeing a large gap between what your organization could be doing and is doing now, between its potential and its reality. Others may have given up and become part of the malaise. What can you do?

Consider how your own growth and well-being could be enhanced by tackling a problem in the organization, how you could become bigger as a person by matching your own stretch to the organizational need. Usually, the things which most alarm or disgust us in an organization are things which echo in some way inside ourselves. Perhaps, after much struggle, you overcame an inclination to gossip and tear others down. That might be the thing which most bothers you in the culture of the organization. If you want to tackle it, consider how you can at the same time clean up the work that remains inside yourself on that issue. There is a lot of empowerment waiting for you if you tackle organizational change in this way, and also a win/win: whether or not you catalyze as big a change in the organization as you'd like, you make progress by becoming a more effective social change agent and joyous human being. That, in turn, will win you allies for your next change effort.

Notes

1. Some of these are: *Z Magazine, The Nation, The Progressive, In These Times, Sojourners, Peacework,* and *National Catholic Reporter.* Fortunately, some periodicals specifically address mass media shortcomings, like *FAIR* and *Adbusters.* The Swiss writer Michele Burdet put the picture starkly: "A recent long visit to California and New England reconfirmed for me how narrow a window on the world is provided by U.S. media. Newspapers and television coverage is wretched. Americans are really miserably informed about what's going on in the world." *Whole Earth Review* #60 (Fall 1988), p. 35.
2. See, for example, ed. Ed Hedemann, *War Resisters League Organizer's Manual* (New York: War Resisters League, 1981) and Kim Bobo, Jackie Kendall, and Steve Max, *Organizing for Social Change* (Washington: Seven Locks Press, 1991).
3. Books which give empowering perspectives include Aldon Morris, *The Origins of the Civil Rights Movement* (New York: The Free Press, 1984); Howard Zinn, *The People's History of the United States* (New York: Harper and Row, 1980); Jeremy Brecher, *Strike* (Boston: South End Press, 1980); James Draper, ed., *Citizen Participation in Canada* (Toronto: New Press, 1971); Robert Cooney and Helen Michalowski, *The Power of the People* (Philadelphia and Gabriola Island, B.C.: New Society Publishers, 1987); Ronald Liversedge, *Recollections of the On to Ottawa Trek* (Toronto: McClelland and Stewart, 1973).
4. Virginia Coover, et al, *Resource Manual for a Living Revolution* (Philadelphia and Gabriola Island, B.C.: New Society Publishers, 1977).
5. See *The Autobiography of Malcolm X*, with Alex Haley (New York: Ballantine, 1973), pp. 340–41: Harvard Sitkoff, *The Struggle for Black Equality 1954–1980* (New York: Hill and Wang, 1981), p. 211; David J. Garrow, *Bearing the Cross: Martin Luther King, Jr., and the Southern Christian Leadership Conference* (New York: William Morrow, 1986), pp. 392–393.

PART IV

FACING THE BOULDERS

What are the features of an organization that make the difference between adequate achievement of goals and excellence? We discuss four: increasing the diversity of backgrounds adds perspective and energy; bringing up and resolving conflicts increases productivity and creativity; spreading negotiation skills through the organization increases balance and empowerment; and using specific techniques to counter burnout supports the well-being of everyone.

Chapter 12

DEVELOPING STRENGTH THROUGH DIVERSITY

Diversity of Background Provides Needed Perspective and Energy

W HEN PEOPLE EMBARK ON AN ORGANIZATIONAL JOURNEY, THEY BRING with them the social inequalities they were brought up with. Society divides people into status groups: some are more valuable than others. White people rank higher than people of color, and the deeper the color, the lower the rank. Men have a higher rank than women, youth is valued over age (except for children), physically and mentally challenged people are marginalized, Christians rank above Jews or Muslims, and people in same gender relationships are seen as flawed. Poor people are treated as worthless no matter how hard they work, while people of means are admired and catered to regardless of how they acquired their wealth or what they do with it.

These different valuations show up as personal prejudices and are woven into the fabric of our culture and our organizations, as power differentials and as ways we experience and understand the world. No one is immune to the biases inherent in their upbringing and culture.[1]

Social change groups usually work on one or two problem areas, and understandably want to focus on their goals and not bother about other issues. It's like the rafters wanting to get unity of focus for the next stretch of white water, and not get sidetracked with the relationships between people on the raft. The trouble is, however, that people don't do their best when their best is discounted because of misperceptions of others on the team. When resources inherent in different backgrounds and perspectives are overlooked, a team's

158

effectiveness suffers. As a result, the team is less able to navigate safely through the white water or to deal creatively with problems that crop up during everyday paddling.

Actually, the rafting metaphor understates the problem. In ongoing organizational life, much more than in a day on the river, the highest quality teamwork under stress simply won't exist without dealing with diversity. For one thing, along with differences come a variety of perspectives, which gives a richer base for perceiving and understanding the situation and coming up with creative and successful solutions. One reason for many of the institutional problems we see in Western culture is that decisions are still being made by a homogeneous group of middle- and upper-class white men. Today's world is much too complicated to be handled by a homogeneous group, no matter how many credentials they may have![2]

Not only is it important to make use of all the human resources in an organization in order to avoid crashing against boulders in the stream, if the goal is a society that is just and that maximizes human potential, it is also necessary to get rid of the oppressive programming that ranks some groups of people higher than others. Working for a goal and undermining it at the same time through members' relations with each other is an obvious contradiction; reducing the contradiction increases effectiveness.

One Way to Work with Diversity Is to Build It Into Your Organization from the Start

This means being very intentional in developing the group that will form the core of a new project or organization. It usually means making contact with people beyond your own circle and being willing to spend more time in the development stage than would otherwise be necessary.

This is not simply a numbers game of recruiting people different from you to support your own agenda. Because our culture gets inside our heads and restricts our vision, it is necessary to reach out to people with different life experiences and probe for their assumptions, getting a look at the issue from their perspectives. It means having a dialogue about how the project or organization shifts when it is enriched by a variety of people bringing their whole selves to the table.[3]

Expect resistance inside yourself to this process. After all, when we passionately want to start a project, we're likely to be very attached to our picture of the goals, the methods, and the special contribution it makes to social change. "Activists are value driven," consultants say, and this can actually make it more difficult for activists to diversify than for the army or for a business. The very attachment to a vision makes it tough to open up the process and do joint creation. Facing this resistance honestly can yield great rewards. Don't brush it off!

Some of my biggest lessons in organizing came from confronting how much I didn't want to change my conception of a project. That was hard because part of me said I am very humble and one of the World's Greatest Listeners, and would surely be flexible about a new effort. The reality was I was dug in: I'd really thought through everything very carefully, and I'm an experienced activist, and there was good reason for every single detail of the project, and why make the project less effective just to cater to others' off-the-top opinions?

Then I happened to go to a diversity workshop and for the first time realized I was really attached, and my attitude might be resistance to an invitation to 'come out and play' with others—out where I felt less secure and less confident. God, I sweated that out! The trust issues that came up— deep down I really didn't trust others to be as smart as me or have as legitimate experience. And I also didn't trust myself to be able to be in a free-flowing dialogue where I could persuade about some things and be persuaded about others. I didn't really feel all that powerful with these people so different from me. So holding onto my marbles (and reminding myself I could take them home) was a natural defensive reaction.

My projects are more successful now because I've learned more about how to listen and understand and stay relaxed. And a really funny byproduct happened. I found that I'd been pouring all my creativity into my work, and one reason why each detail was so important to me was the same way a composer would feel about each note or a painter about each stroke. So I went back to writing poems, which I used to do in college, and I can obsess about them as much as I want to, and get them to be a complete and perfect expression of me. And the organizing work I can be more relaxed about—so I'm better at it, too.

—a veteran white male organizer

If Your Organization Already Exists, Conduct a Diversity Assessment

The objective is to identify areas where change is needed and create a timeline and bench marks against which to evaluate progress. It can be done any time, but is especially relevant as part of a strategic planning process.

The assessment includes gathering demographic data about people who participate in the group's work at different levels: board, staff, volunteers, members, and clients. Gender, racial, and ethnic identity are basic in most situations. Others that might be relevant for your group are age, religion, income level, sexual orientation, and ability.[4]

In addition to demographics, ask:

- What kind of recruitment or outreach is done? Where and to whom?
- What do your descriptive materials say about who you are in terms of diversity?
- How are new people in different parts of the organization oriented? (Note: what assumptions do you make about what new people need to know?)
- How do people find out what is going on, formally and informally?
- What are the expectations and experiences of the different people involved?
- What do outsiders think of the organization, particularly people from groups that are not represented in your organization?

You can gather responses through well-designed questionnaires, focus groups, individual interviews, or a combination of methods. Interviews and focus groups work best if conducted by someone who is not part of the organization. An outsider is less likely to have an axe to grind, and more likely to notice what is not said as well as what is said.

Analysis of the responses is as important as asking the questions. In what ways do people from different identity groups see things differently from each other? Women and men usually experience an organization in different ways, and African American women often see things differently from European American women. The same holds for men. Majority group people in the organization often complain that minority group people huddle in cliques, not realizing that from the other side they may be seen the same way. Because a lot of organizational information travels through informal routes, different groups often have different information about what is going on. Addtionally, everyone interprets information in terms of its context and their own place in that context, so different groups may draw different conclusions from the same information.[5]

To build trust in the process, don't have the analysis of the responses performed by existing organizational leaders. Get an outside facilitator, or create a committee which is itself representative. Remember, this is sensitive information that has an emotional charge.

> **A large environmental organization hired a consultant to do a careful diversity assessment and then put his report on the shelf in the executive director's office, where it gathered dust. The mystery report became the focus of suspicion and resentment, especially among those who participated in the assessment. When repeated promises to share the report didn't materialize, cynicism grew and the diversity work in the organization took a large step backwards.**
>
> —*a consultant to the organization*

Delving into diversity is exploring the shadow side of Western culture, and of activist culture. Expect people to get uncomfortable and defensive at times. The credibility of the guide, be this a person or a committee, may be crucial to the outcome of the analysis.

An important part of the process is reporting back to the people who participated what was found and what recommendations are being developed. The reporting process becomes the first step in change, because it provides an opportunity for people to talk about issues that otherwise are not dealt with in a structured way. Reporting also demonstrates that the leadership takes the process seriously.

Organizations learning from their diversity assessment usually find that they need to increase the number of participants from certain groups, in some or all parts of their work. A health care reform group may have a majority of women as members but mostly men on the board. An antipoverty group may have an essentially young, white staff while serving mostly elderly black people. A youth service program may appear to have a diverse staff, but on closer examination has a largely black and Latino support staff and a white program staff. A neighborhood improvement group may realize that Latino families have moved into the neighborhood over the past several years but none of them have become involved in the organization. An environmental group may be all white despite the fact that chemical pollution is especially present in neighborhoods where there are practically no white people.

Create an Aggressive, Thoughtful Recruitment Strategy

The clarity and breadth of your strategy will show whether or not your organization understands the need. Half-hearted recruitment results in lack of qualified candidates. "We can't find qualified people" is a lame excuse by now. In recruiting for diversity:

- take the time to find out where to look,
- realize that your organization probably has little credibility with the people among whom you are recruiting (which may reflect lack of preparedness for diversity and multiculturalism),
- don't have different standards for the group you are recruiting (i.e., don't look for individuals who walk on water),
- make certain that all criteria are relevant and necessary,
- be careful not to disregard people who don't "speak our language," people who make you uncomfortable because you are unfamiliar with their ways,[6]
- if there is a shortage of people of the group you are seeking in your field or geographical area, take into account that additional training or incentives may be necessary.

Keep these points in mind when recruiting for increased participation from under-represented groups:

Don't rely on personal contacts: they are too limited. Go to where the people are that you are trying to interest. Educate yourself on how they see the world. Contact leaders of community groups, churches, professional associations, etc. Find ways to develop relationships with

163

A 1992 story in the Washington Journalism Review quotes a managing editor of a daily newspaper in California where all newsroom staff was white, but where they would "very much like to have minorities on staff." She says that they don't get resumes from minorities but that they also do not recruit for positions.

The story also recounts the experience of another California managing editor who was able to increase the number of minorities on staff from four per cent to twenty per cent in two years by going to job fairs in nearby big cities.[7]

them and their groups. Look for ways you can develop common cause.

Be clear about what you have to offer as an organization and what you are looking for from potential members or staff. Never make the mistake of saying what you want is "the women's point of view" or "the black perspective," since no community can be represented by just a few voices.

Avoid tokenism. People who are in a minority carry a heavy burden because they nearly always feel (and usually with good reason) that their performance will reflect on their whole group. They also have to deal with the fact that other people don't quite know how to relate to them. Some people will be patronizing while others seemingly ignore them or assume they have little to contribute to issues under discussion. It's a rare person who will stick around in a situation where her or his presence makes other people uncomfortable.

In a sizable peace and justice organization there was persistent trouble building up a substantial participation on the board of people of color, even though the staff was racially integrated. Even though a new board member was sincerely interested in the group's work, after a time she stopped coming to meetings when it became clear to her that she had been invited to join the board as the token minority person. Eventually, she resigned. Not until the organization opened a number of board spots for people of color did the turnover stop and the board become diverse.

—former executive director

164

Agree to be Honest without Calling Each Other Names

Many organizations have slowed down their progress on diversity by creating a culture which allows name-calling: "racist," "sexist," "anti-Semitic," etc. The problem with name-calling is it manages to be insulting while stating the obvious. Of course people in the group are racist, or sexist—the culture has conditioned everyone to be that way. One would have to be literally from another planet not to be. Idealism does not immunize anyone from the effects of conditioning that starts in infancy and is practically part of the air we breathe.

To complicate the matter even more, most people who have experienced oppression have internalized the messages, which invites us to use name-calling to avoid dealing with our own low self-esteem. There can be a feeling of righteous satisfaction—however fleeting—when we've labelled someone else with an attitude that we also share inside.

Racism and the other "isms" are a kind of cultural pollution, a poison set loose in the environment that we all experience. It's as if a town has discovered, after many years, that there is an old toxic waste dump on its outskirts that is leaking into the water supply. Everyone is affected to some degree. The question for the townspeople is: is it useful to feel guilty about the pollution, or to take responsibility, roll up their sleeves, and change the situation?

Name-calling is about blame and guilt. It may be an improvement over denying that oppressive patterns operate in the organization, but not much of an improvement. The following fictional example may sound familiar:

CRYSTAL: "I can't believe you did that—you're a sexist."

CHARLIE: "What do you mean? I am not!"

CRYSTAL: "Yes, you are. I felt completely disrespected when you picked up my suggestion in the meeting and got it through as if it was your own."

CHARLIE: "I was only doing what would work to get your proposal through! You know I'm not sexist! I do respect you, and I fight for your ideas because I know they're good."

Charlie is being defensive and refusing to listen carefully for the learning potential in Crystal's feedback. He hears Crystal's charge as

165

an invitation to feel guilty—a feeling few of us like to feel. Crystal, by labelling Charlie a sexist, is stating the obvious, making Charlie defensive, and frustrating herself at the same time. It is genuinely useful for the organization to identify behaviors and patterns which are ageist, homophobic, etc., by looking at their results:

CRYSTAL: "Charlie, I'd like you to look at something that happened in the meeting today and see how it could be handled differently another time."

CHARLIE: "What happened?"

CRYSTAL: "Remember when I made that suggestion for the fundraising drive, and then later you picked up on it and persuaded everyone we should do it? Your advocating the idea did get it through, but it reinforces the assumption around here that it's men's ideas that really count. And it was personally upsetting to me. When you pick up an idea of mine and run with it as if it's yours, I feel ignored and invisible, because it's like my intelligence isn't worth much because I'm a woman. I'd like you to see what that's like from my point of view."

Crystal is talking about consequences: Charlie's behavior reinforced a sexist pattern in meetings and also led to her personally feeling ignored and invisible. As their conversation continues she can continue to focus on results and ask him to consider how he could behave in a way that wouldn't produce those results. At some point, if it becomes useful, she could label the behavior "sexist" and expect Charlie to understand what she means by that, because they have already been talking about the results of the behavior being named.

People like Crystal and Charlie need and deserve assistance from the organization, beyond ground rules like "No name-calling." Workshops on communication or conflict resolution in diversity situations can give practical help. Such training may be especially important for supervisors and leaders who have responsibility for ensuring a healthy organizational climate. Specific suggestions relevant to diversity can be found in many chapters in this book.

Create Identity Groups to Support Your Group's Work on Diversity

Bringing together identity groups give people a chance to compare notes with others to make sure they are not "going crazy," to express anger as well as amusement, and to think about how to bring about change. It's easier for Crystal in the above story to deal with Charlie knowing that she has a group of supportive women to listen to her and her feelings. She knows she doesn't have to vent her upset with him, and instead can focus on dealing with him and the sexist practices in the organization in an effective way. An identity group also identifies differences between people belonging to the same group, and provides a safer place in which to deal with problems between people in the group.

Healthy identity groups are places where people grow, individually and as a group, in claiming their strengths and recognizing their weaknesses; they are not only for complaining and blaming, which beyond a certain point is an exercise in powerlessness.

Organizations may be wise to allocate the resources needed for identity groups to develop skills for positive change. Such resources include time, access to occasional training or work with a consultant, publications, etc.[8]

This national organization had a commitment to diversity on paper, yet it remained predominantly white, with a cultural tone of "New England/California new left anti-authority activism." The people of color turned to each other in frustration and started to meet over meal breaks during national conferences. After a while, they announced the formation of a people of color caucus, and in a plenary session demanded that quality time be set aside for them to meet. Emotions rose as whites made stirring (and defensive) pleas for unity. The highly-respected national chair tipped the balance by explaining the value and role of identity groups, acknowledging that issues of power were on the table, and lifting up an image of diversity that confronts honestly and realistically the force of inherited patterns of inequality. The conference voted to meet the caucus's demands.

For a period of three years following that pivotal meeting, the organization made rapid progress in diversifying. Specific goals were made and met, the organizational culture became richer, and the organizational

167

structure, *including supervision and decision-making, became clearer, tighter, and more efficient. Most of the reforms were initiated by the people of color caucus, which customarily made its report near the beginning of the national meeting (after having flown in early to have its own meetings) and often made needed proposals for changes in organizational practices and structure, as well as specific diversity proposals. The caucus also disciplined one of its members who was race-baiting to avoid measuring up on his job. The white people became used to dealing with racial issues that were fraught with emotion and tensions about power, and became less defensive and more aware of their own racism. They also experienced the rich satisfactions of working in an organization they didn't "have to" control but where they could instead be partners.*

—member of the executive committee of the organization during this period

An identity group must be flexible enough to recognize that each individual represents a complex set of identities.[9] A woman also has a racial or ethnic identity, and may be lesbian, bisexual or heterosexual, and may have a strong religious tradition. White women and women of color have things in common, yet there are also important aspects of their lives and places in society that make them different from each other and at times at odds with each other. The same complexity is true for men. Ignoring these differences can add to the tension; on the other hand, no organization can deal with everything at one time. An organization which acknowledges the variety of what are known as "oppression/liberation issues," then proceeds to focus attention on one at a time, will learn valuable lessons from each encounter to apply to the next.

Working on Diversity Sooner Is Better

Inequalities and dominating behavior show up especially during crises or under the stress of deadlines. Those may not be the best times to resolve conflicts. Wise leaders work on diversity before the crisis. It also helps to set aside time as soon as possible after a crisis to look at what happened and identify what needs to change.

Since few groups started out as multicultural organizations, most have yet to learn that the needed changes are deep and have rich potential. It is a serious mistake to think that all that's needed is for "a few of them to join us." Diversity is not about "them" becoming like "us," it is about all of us becoming new creatures, who in some ways will be different and who may make different choices. For people used to being in control, this is an unsettling realization. Work on getting over it.[10]

Instead of Feeling Overwhelmed, Try Collaboration

The bad news, for a tired leader, is to realize that everything is connected to everything else. The good news, for a tired leader, is to realize that everything is *connected* to everything else. Connectedness can fuel efforts at collaboration and mutual support between organizations working on different issues, or similar issues from a different angle.

Collaborations can strengthen the work of each group and therefore serve the goal of creating a more just and caring world. For example, the cause of antiracism could be furthered by collaborative neighborhood projects involving churches with different racial identities, or by the active support of a white educational advocacy group working with a Latino parents group in their children's school. However, this will succeed only on certain conditions:

- If serious efforts are made by the white groups to educate themselves about the worldview and conditions that are shared by members of the other group.
- If whites educate each other about the dynamics of institutionalized racism.
- If whites refrain from telling the other group what to do.
- If whites remember to ask what form of support would be most helpful.

Otherwise, the collaboration will be experienced as another example of white paternalism.[11] The members of a white organization will make it much more likely that their group will change into a multiracial organization by taking responsibility to understand the reality of other groups, as well as by acknowledging the ways in which they have themselves been affected by racism.[12]

Don't Take It Out on Each Other!

Distrust and wariness of each other are common between members of groups which have suffered bias and discrimination. Sometimes the competition is expressed in fights about theory: class oppression is more basic than gender oppression, for example. Rivalries for "victim chic" reveal a fundamental bias in the worldview promoted by our culture: everything should be ranked on a vertical scale. We're taught by parents, peers, school, and the media to compare everything as better than/worse than, more attractive/less attractive, superior/inferior, more significant/less significant. Men are taught to rate women's attractiveness on a scale of one to ten, we rate our movies, our cities, politicians, books, ideas, and sexual experiences. This is not our fault; we're simply brought up with a habit of mind which makes continual judgements of comparison. How predictable, then, that we would rank oppressions, assume that there must be a primary oppression or that the group we are part of has been most badly abused.

Fortunately, there is another way of seeing besides vertical ranking. Once conscious of the vertical habit of mind, we can deliberately ask "How would these look if they were arranged horizontally? If the movies I see, to use an everyday example, are not better than or worse than each other but have some things in common and some different, use ideas in certain ways and not in other ways, etc?"

A horizontal framework applied to group identity, instead of asking who is most oppressed, asks how the identities interconnect, how they are different, how their experiences provide opportunities for alliance, and how they contradict each other and reinforce each other.

> One of the bigger nonprofits in the city has hired a lot of minorities over the years, but I wouldn't want to work there because of the attitude I run into where each minority competes for points on how oppressed it is. It's like there's a kind of victim chic. Too many people use their victimhood to score points in the political battles that happen.
>
> —*a gay man in a large Eastern city*

Of course there are times in life when vertical ranking is useful, but in this culture rating is an unconscious compulsion, and unconscious compulsions are by definition antiliberation—not to mention how they prevent the celebration of diversity.[13]

Don't Expect Overnight Transformation

Most of the oppressions we experience have taken thousands of years to root themselves, so it may take more than six months—or six years—to overcome them. Building trust takes time and involves risk on everyone's part, especially when old power relationships have to be rearranged and new behaviors learned. Patience and perseverence are needed for rafting on this river.[14]

Mistakes will be made on all sides. Rather than explaining and defending the mistakes, it is better to acknowledge them and express regrets to those who have been affected. Then figure out together how to do better in the future. The only way not to make any mistakes in this area is to do nothing, which is the biggest mistake of all.

Diversity is the practice of valuing the unique strengths and perspectives that people bring from their backgrounds. Like other forms of freedom, it is worth the struggle.

Notes

1. Richard H. Brown, "Cultural Representation and Ideological Domination," *Social Forces*, 71:3, March 1993.
2. For information on how that plays out in one important arena, see Donald Snow, *Inside the Environmental Movement: Meeting the Leadership Challenge* (Washington, D.C.: Island Press, 1992).
3. The Girl Scouts of the U.S.A. commissioned a revealing study to learn how better to serve a more diverse population in terms of race, ethnicity, and class; see the report by Sumry Erkut, Jacqueline Fields, Deirdre Almeida, Brunilda DeLeaon, Rachel Sing, and Stephanie Geller, *There is Diversity within Diversity: Community Leaders' Views on Increasing Diversity in Youth-Serving Organizations* (Wellseley College: Research Center on Women, 1993).
4. In her well-known book, *Men and Women of the Corporation*, (New York: Basic Books, 1977), Rosabeth Moss Kanter describes three variables that help explain how individuals behave in an organization: "the structure of opportunity, the structure of power, and the proportional distribution of people of different kinds

171

(the social composition of peer clusters)," p. 245.

5. See bell hooks, *Feminist Theory: From Margin to Center* (Boston: South End Press, 1984). In her preface, hooks discusses how people who find themselves at the center of society rarely have "knowledge and awareness of men and women who live in the margin. As a consequence [their] theory lacks wholeness, lacks the broad analysis that could encompass a variety of human experience."

6. A lively book of drawings and text, which offers a helpful review nearly everyone can use, is *Filtering People: Understanding and Confronting Our Prejudices*, by Jim Cole (Philadelphia and Gabriola Island, B.C.: New Society Publishers, 1990).

7. Katherine Corcoran, "Reaching for Diversity," *Washington Journalism Review*, July/August 1992, pp. 38–42.

8. A variety of useful publications have come from identity groups and their spin-offs. See, for example, *Bridges of Respect: Creating Support for Lesbian and Gay Youth* (Philadelphia: American Friends Service Committee, 1989); and Gerald L. Mallon, ed., *Resisting Racism: An Action Guide* (San Francisco: National Association of Black and White Men Together, 1991).

9. Patricia Williams, who wrote the book *The Alchemy of Race and Rights: A Diary of a Law Professor* (Cambridge, Mass.: Harvard University Press, 1991) is the great-granddaughter of a slave and her white master (who was a lawyer). She writes, "My attempts to write in my own voice have placed me in the center of a snarl of social tensions and cross boundaries." (p. 6).

10. Increasingly, useful articles can be found in popular media. In 1991, forexample, *Working Woman* did a special report on cultural diversity including "The Enlightened Manager: How to Treat all your Employees Fairly," and "Twelve Companies that do the Right Thing," January 1991, pp. 45–60.

11. Long-time southern organizer Anne Braden emphasizes the importance of white groups' internal education on racism; see her article "Un-doing Racism: Lessons for the Peace Movement" in *The Nonviolent Activist*, April–May, 1987, pp. 3–6. A valuable resource for this purpose is *America's Original Sin: A Study Guide on White Racism*, (Washington: Sojourners Magazine, 1988).

12. This is documented by diversity consultant Andrea Ayvazian in her unpublished Ph.D. dissertation, *Partners in Justice: A Concerned White Person's Guide to Combatting Racism*, (Graduate School of the Union Institute, 1994). Dr. Ayvazian is Director of Communitas, Inc., 245 Main St., Northampton, MA 01060.

13. This discussion of vertical and horizontal thinking draws from the work of Riane Eisler, *The Chalice and the Blade* (New York: Harper and Row, 1988). An ironic aspect of activists ranking each others' oppression is that this way of thinking duplicates, in form, the prejudice in the larger society to which we referred in the beginning of this chapter.

14. With a longer-term perspective, organizers begin to get satisfaction and enjoyment from weaving into the organization's life the practices that reflect consciousness on diversity. For ideas on how to do this, see the brief handbook "Interactive Exercises: Skills Building through Participation" compiled by staff at the Center for Community Change, 1000 Wisconsin Ave., NW, Washington, DC 20007.

Chapter 13

DEALING WITH CONFLICT

Every group and every relationship has conflicts within it; conflict is as natural as breathing. Groups that handle conflict well get stronger as a result. A group or relationship that is so new that it hasn't yet worked through a conflict is a fragile enterprise. It needs to face conflict to become strong.

People who are out to change the world in some way often find themselves in conflict with the powers-that-be. One might think that they are comfortable with conflict among themselves. Not so—many activists are champion conflict-avoiders. Political and cultural differences, frustrations with the work, dynamic personalities, and sensitivity over authority issues can create a climate of discontent in organizations. Instead of dealing with tensions as they occur, people tend to wait until there is an explosion and stored up conflicts threaten to blow the entire organization apart.

For a time an organization may hold together even while avoiding internal conflicts, through the excitement of its vision and its struggle with the forces of the status quo. However, just as successful long-term love relationships are not built on vacations, honeymoons, or other extraordinary events, a social change organization does not remain successful over the long haul from its occasional times in the limelight or short-term victories. Long-term relationships and effective groups develop by continually working through their differences.

This chapter offers a variety of approaches to making conflict resolution a healthy and creative part of organizational life. Many organizations already use some of them. Any organization could

> *Most of the time what has worked has been building a structure that values that role [of conflict facilitator]. I once gave an interview to a newspaper where they called me a practitioner of permanent revolution. I talked to them about building structures that are constantly checking in with people and encouraging people to articulate minority positions so that you make the rebel part of your bureaucracy. I use this because that is basically what a good rank and file union is. If you are really going to have participatory democracy then you have to have people differing. If the leadership is giving conscious, responsible value to that struggle needing to occur within the organization and there are structures that will allow people to struggle with each other on principles, then you have an organization willing to change in fundamental ways on a regular basis. It is easier than to isolate those people who are rebellious in irresponsible ways or maybe are right but can't get anybody to support them.*
>
> —an experienced union and community action leader

benefit from using conflict resolution tools such as these to prevent energy from being wasted on internal resentments rather than being focused on the organization's mission.

Acknowledge That Conflict Is Often Avoided

In the early stages of a successful social movement, a small, struggling minority typically raises tough issues the majority of the population does not want to face. The activists may be maligned, unappreciated, and sometimes even victimized by the society they are attempting to heal. Already in tension with the powerholders and sometimes with the mainstream, they hate to add to that discomfort by acknowledging conflicts among themselves.

Further, many activists are brought up in a society which is not especially skillful at dealing with conflicts. Like other people, activists often lack certain valuable interpersonal skills. The pressures of moving their cause forward through a world that is often hostile or indifferent breed conflict in the ranks. Yet, because they want to maintain a sense of harmony, they often deny and avoid facing conflict. This has resulted in more than one progressive organization splitting or self-destructing.

An important activist trait is pointing out truths when society is in denial. In the same way, activists need to look honestly at their own organizations and acknowledge that conflict avoidance is a problem.

Build Trust

A group of twenty-five veteran activists from a variety of cultures around the United States was recently asked: "What is the single most important ingredient for building a successful organization?"

The answer: "Trust."

The concept of trust can be formulated as an equation:

$$\text{Trust} = \frac{\text{Intimacy} \ \times \ \text{Competence}}{\text{Degree of Risk}}$$

This equation presents the trust level in your organization as the result of elements which act interdependently. Intimacy has to do with closeness of relationships in the group. Competency has to do with the skills and knowledge needed for performing an organizational role or getting the job done.

You can use this equation to evaluate the trust level in your organization, or the amount of trust people have in you or another individual, by using the following procedure. It is based on subjective perception, but even though subjective it works fine for diagnosis. By using this method, you'll also come up with ideas on how to build trust.

Intimacy is composed of five variables:

1. Degree of affection felt. Trust your gut on this one.
2. Degree of collaboration. How easy is it to work together without competing for status or power?
3. Ease with conflict. How much is it OK to disagree and challenge?
4. Disclosure. How much does the individual or group hold back information on their intentions and plans?
5. Predictability. Consistency increases confidence.

175

Rate the organization or the individual by placing them on a 1 to 10 scale (1 is low, 10 is high) on each of the variables. For example, you might give a 7 for affection, a 6 for collaboration, a 2 for conflict. Add the five scores for the intimacy variables and divide by five, and that is the general intimacy score.

Multiply the general intimacy score by the score for competence. In this case, competence is the degree that you perceive the group or individual as skilled in the mission or role that they have. In measuring my supervisor, for example, I would measure her on a 1 to 10 scale in terms of competence at supervision, not at being my friend or as a political thinker; my focus would be role-specific. The multiplication of the general intimacy score by the competency score results in a number somewhere between 1 and 100.

Divide the number just computed by the score for degree of risk, which represents how much risk there is in the relationship. If I am measuring trust with regard to my supervisor, then degree of risk would probably relate to the likelihood that the supervisor could or would fire me, reject me, or limit my influence in the organization. Most often, risk is related to rejection. If there is a high degree of risk that an individual or group could or would reject me, and this could have major consequences for my life, then the degree of risk would be high, demanding a high score. If, on the other hand, the risk is low that I would be rejected or hurt, then the score is low. (In this variable, it is better to have a low score than a high one.)

By dividing the number you got through multiplying intimacy and competency by the score you gave to degree of risk, you get a number for trust level. The number is subjective, and yet it can be useful if you compare it with a later evaluation you do in the same way to see whether the trust level is going up or down. Most important, by being honest with each of the variables in the equation, you can see the areas of needed development within the organization or with your own relationships within the organization. The very process of thinking it through will clarify your options.

It can be powerful to have a subgroup in your organization (board, staff, or committee) complete this equation anonymously and then compile the score, using it as a dignostic and team-building device. You may want to have a skilled outside facilitator do this with you, to assist in discussing the issues raised and developing next steps in building trust. Discovering why members have a low level of trust may bring up a lot of defensiveness and could escalate problems if not handled well. When groups identify the areas which reduce trust and have the time and structure to be thoughtful, they often realize what it will take to increase the trust and can recommend specific and valuable strategies for increasing their trust in each of the identified areas. Using the measure periodically as a stimulus for discussion and growth can hold a group accountable for its own efforts toward change.

Establish Ground Rules and Check In

Over time, every group creates a set of norms or rules, which govern how the organization operates and how members interact. Many of the norms are quite unconscious, and most are never discussed, just assumed. This may lead to people receiving mixed messages about what is expected of them, judgementalism, and resentment. An organization's culture may condone discriminatory practices and lead to the isolation of minority views and emotions.

An alternative to the unspoken rules is to reach agreements on what ground rules will guide the way people work and communicate together. A good place to start clarifying ground rules is in meetings. Based on the goals, time available, and participants present, decide what structure is necessary to keep the flow of discussion open and bring out the wisdom in the group. In the beginning, if the meeting is to last more than an hour, try agreeing ahead of time to take five minutes out, thirty to sixty minutes into the meeting, to check on how people feel about their participation and whether or not the ground rules are being honored. Amazingly, just knowing that the group will stop and look at itself will prompt most participants to act more responsibly. During the five-minute check-in a larger conflict might surface, and you can schedule a time to resolve it, or work with it on the spot. (See chapter 9 for more suggestions about handling conflicts in meetings.)

From starting with meeting ground rules, norms can be extended throughout the organization. A group might decide that not enough conflict is coming into the open because people are afraid of personal attacks, so a ground rule could be adopted that criticism of ideas is fine, but not of individuals. A group might want to challenge racist and other oppressive behaviors without producing a climate of fear where members are tiptoeing around afraid they might say or do something wrong. The group could adopt a guideline that shows how to challenge while still respecting the integrity of the person and the reality that we all make mistakes.

This may sound perfectly reasonable, but developing norms into practiced behaviors often requires skill sessions or workshops where the new practices are given clear attention and the ground rules are legitimized. If listening, for example, is valued, it should not be assumed that people know how to listen well or that listening will improve just because the group affirms its importance. Old habits die hard, and a workshop or other forms of practice may be needed, so that momentum develops and makes the listening ground rule viable.

A national environmental organization was having trouble with unresolved internal conflicts: some were chronic and nasty, others were avoided until explosions occurred and valued participants left. To counteract the dread that some of the leaders were feeling about the annual meeting, a consultant was asked to facilitate the event.

The consultant spent the first day of the retreat teaching conflict resolution and group dynamics skills to the leaders, suggesting that these new skills be practiced for the rest of the retreat. The leaders did so, and found they could handle difficult issues in a sensitive and productive way.

On the last day, the leaders wrote a group letter to the rest of the organization requesting that new ground rules be implemented throughout the organization which would increase respect and effectiveness. Follow-up skill-building workshops were then planned.

—the consultant who worked with the organization

Retreats for setting goals and planning can be used to build skills that use differences for creative outcomes.

Listen Best When It's Hardest

A long-experienced Native American organizer found listening to be the key in dealing with a rebel in her community:

I understood that this man had perspective and a thread of reality that I needed to pay attention to and sift through. There was always something there that brought clarity to the situation. I admired him because he was tenacious (though a real pain). I learned to respect him—his strong emotions were real and had to be listened to and dealt with. You can't take these three minute segments with Indian culture. You need to acknowledge elders, have to hear people out and eventually you get cohesive. Have to throw away the clock: "We won't leave until we figure this out." Maintain respect for everyone (including the jerks), knowing that from the most unlikely sources you'll get enlightenment. Throw away ego.

Most of us think we are good listeners. We pride ourselves on our ability to take in information and listen to what is being said. Why is it, then, that if you go into almost any organization and ask people to put on a scale of 1 to 10 the degree to which they feel "heard," the score is low?

People who do not feel heard usually become frustrated, agitated, belligerent, passive, resistant, or in some other way dysfunctional. On the other hand, it is difficult for people to stay angry when they feel they are being listened to. To feel heard is to feel cared for. This is why successful relationships do not require agreement as much as they require understanding. Organizations, too, can tolerate a great deal of disagreement and difference if there is a high degree of understanding on the part of those who differ. This is a source of optimism for leaders who want broad diversity of backgrounds in their organizations.

Based on past experience a lot of us don't expect to be heard. As a result we often go on the attack by overtalking and interrupting to ensure that we have been heard. Instead of really listening, we are actively preparing our rebuttal and impatiently waiting for the other person to take a breath so we can add our latest argument. Just as in most wars, the conflict doesn't actually get resolved. Yet we will almost certainly repeat this pattern the next time such a situation arises.

What's the alternative? If one person allows, or even encourages, the other to vent the feelings that are behind the words and shows that she or he has fully heard what has been communicated before responding, real dialogue can happen. Good listening will invariably reframe the context of the fight.

The key to what has been called active or empathic listening is the ability to reflect back the essence of the content and feelings being shared by the other person. Mechanical repeating of the words of the other will not do; you need to paraphrase the critical ideas and feelings being expressed to show that you have truly understood.

This does not require sainthood on anyone's part. It is possible to be frustrated and angry oneself and still be empathic in listening to another person. Being empathic is the act of successfully communicating to the other party that you have understood both the information and the feelings that are being communicated. It takes concentrated effort and focused attention not to get defensive and let our own feelings get in the way of hearing what is being said.

The discipline of restraining yourself from quickly responding before the person has expressed her or his feelings makes listening effective The following example of a heated argument shows how active listening works.

BARBARA: "What drives me crazy in this situation is your feeling that you always have to be right! You always act so sure of yourself. If I differ with you, it immediately turns into a win-lose situation and a fight. Right now, for example, we were beginning to discuss the possibility of a demonstration in front of the mayor's office. You dismissed it out of hand. You're so goddamned sure of everything. And that's only the tip of the iceberg."

MARIA: "It sounds from what you're saying that you feel like you're never heard, and you're obviously really pissed. That feels like the issue, not the demonstration, although clearly you don't feel heard on that issue, either."

BARBARA: "You're damned right! It's just another example, probably the straw that broke my back, and I'm tired of it. As far as I'm concerned, you can take the demonstration and shove it!"

MARIA: "Somehow your anger seems to have been building up and you haven't really shown it to me before."

BARBARA: "That's right. And I've had it up to here!"

MARIA: "If I felt unheard and run over, I'd feel angry, too. But I also believe that whatever is happening, we need to change the situation and not let it happen again. Would you be open to that?"

BARBARA: "Yes, I guess so, but I'm not sure you're going to change."

MARIA: "So, you doubt my intentions, or maybe my ability to change?"

BARBARA: "Yes, it's been going on a long time."

MARIA: "For my part, I do have a tendency to get carried away and to get going too fast. And sometimes, I'm obviously too assertive with my own idea before looking at someone else's. But, I also hope that you will own your part of the problem—shutting down and letting me get away with it! So why don't we take a look at what we both have to do to stop this pattern. I don't want to lose your trust, and I don't want to bottle up my enthusiasm."

Barbara: "Well, I realize I should probably have said something before this and not let it build. But, I never think it's going to do any good, so I just shove it inside."

MARIA: "Until it blows up all over us?"

BARBARA: "That's right, and that can be a pretty stupid way of handling it."

Maria made a conscious effort to focus on Barbara's feelings as well as the difference between them. By focusing and paraphrasing, Maria used only one-third of the the words Barbara did in her initial outburst. Barbara's response to Maria's empathic listening was an affirming "You're damn right!" Having been heard, Barbara again showed anger but more briefly. Maria's response was sensitive, pointed, and showed listening beyond the words that were being spoken. Barbara again responded with an affirmative "That's right" and one last angry "I've had it up to here!" At that point it was fairly easy for Maria to own her part of the problem, while still recognizing that it's a two-way street and both women can share responsibility on the issue. When Barbara admits that it is not only Maria's difficulty, the opportunity for creative problem solving has opened up.

What if Barbara continued being angry, or wanted to punish Maria? Blaming, justifying, or somehow pushing down true feelings would probably escalate the tension and magnify the conflict. Maria's best option might be to retreat for the moment and wait until Barbara cooled down and was more ready to dialogue.

Briefly, empathic or active listening is useful because it legitimizes real feelings, allows catharsis of those feelings, focuses on the differences themselves rather than justification and blame, creates a climate of greater understanding, and moves the confrontation from hostility to problem solving.

While active listening is not a panacea and cannot solve all conflicts by itself, such listening can help sort out what the issues and the stakes actually are. Finding a resolution might require a more specific problem solving process and possibly the assistance of a third party or the involvement of additional people.

Active listening can also be helpful when you are trying to help someone figure out what to do in a difficult situation. Rather than giving advice or walking away, try paraphrasing the thoughts and feelings you hear expressed by the other person. This may gradually help open up new possibilities.

Challenge Gossip and Triangulation

The rumor mill is most profoundly destructive when one person goes to another with the famous "Listen, I want to share something with you, but you have to promise that it won't go beyond you." First of all, chances are that the confidence will spread. Gossiping and rumor mongering allows individuals to take no responsibility for the information they spread. Also, most gossip is in reference to individuals who frequently have no way of protecting themselves from the truth or untruth of the statement. While the gossiping provides a moment of titillation and excitement, in the long run it can weaken the fabric of an organization. Since people who naturally feel comfortable together go to each other, it encourages adversarial relationships and group division.

Another way conflicts turn destructive is through creating triangular communication. Instead of Rasheed going directly to Andre with his irritation about Andre's performance in the news conference, Rasheed complains to Tandra and asks her to deal with Andre. By far the most useful thing for Tandra to do is to refuse and insist that Rasheed tell Andre directly. If he really needs assistance, she might offer to be with Rasheed as a support person. For Tandra to do Rasheed's work for him is disempowering for Rasheed and a serious problem for the organization.[1]

Work Hard and Play Hard

People get into fewer conflicts with people they like, have fun with, and enjoy being around. Organizations which work hard under stressful conditions need periodic respites to relax and to heal. Laughing and playing together give people a chance to see different sides of each other. This makes it easier to see new possibilities in their working relationship. If I can relax with you, it is easier to work out differences without getting into a win-loose situation.

Make Feedback a Regular Organizational Practice

Feedback is essential to an organization that wants its conflicts to be handled creatively and productively. Feedback provides specific and descriptive information about a person's or group's behavior or an event that has occurred, and about its impact on others.

Feedback sounds scary. Try this experiment: walk up to someone you know and say simply, "I'd like to give you a little feedback." Watch the person's face. More than likely, you will see fear or trepidation in their eyes. Usually the assumption is that if I am going to give you feedback, I will tell you about something you did wrong. And to make matters worse, I will probably want you to change something that I don't like.

How did feedback get such a bad reputation? Since people don't generally tell us when we are doing well, but do let us know about our shortcomings, we soon learn that feedback equals criticism. If there is one thing that encourages us to feel defensive and resistant, it is feeling judged or evaluated in a negative way by someone else. Also, most of us have feelings of insecurity and are more ready to hear the bad news than the good.

Feedback Is Not Meant to Be Either Positive or Negative

The receiver of feedback may interpret the information as positive or negative, but the information itself ought to be descriptive and nonjudgemental. Providing such feedback is a skill in short supply, but fortunately it is a learnable skill.

The key to effective feedback is to describe an event or a behavior by using specifics, giving details, and describing the consequences of the event to yourself or others: "When you lost your temper and shouted at us in staff meeting (description) I felt very defensive and did not want to say anything else for the rest of the afternoon." (consequences to yourself) The person may not wish to hear the feedback, but it is unlikely that her or his goal was to shut you up and have you withdraw for the afternoon. The angry person needs to know the consequences of his or her behavior, and the shut down person needs to move away from the disempowering feelings of blame and resentment. Delivering the feedback meets both needs.

"When you go around and around without getting to the point, I get frustrated, find myself not listening, and then I get upset because I think what you have to say may be important." This statement does not interpret what's behind the rambling or resort to judging and name calling. It focuses on the behavior and takes responsibility for the speaker's reactions without asserting who is right and who is wrong. As an "I statement," it follows the simple formula: "When you _____ I feel _____ because _____." It sets the stage for changing behavior or for joint problem solving.

The essence of feedback, then, is not fancy: it is direct, specific, and descriptive. Here are other considerations for giving feedback.

- Feedback works best when it is timely. The closer the feedback is to the event the more helpful it will be, since everyone will more easily remember what happened and what the circumstances were. Also remember, it can be aggravating to realize that someone has had important information for you and held on to it for a long time.
- Be generous with affirming feedback. "When you took the initiative in handling that bully at the demonstration, I felt so much safer and more confident that we'll win our campaign." An organization in which people give each other affirming feedback learns faster and increases its effectiveness, as well as boosts its members' morale.
- Be aware that some people cannot hear affirming feedback. Give it anyway. Some of it may get through eventually.
- Accept that the receiver of your feedback may not change her or his behavior. The nature of feedback is that it leaves the choice of response to the receiver. It is different from a negotiated agreement.
- Find a setting in which the receiver may be most open and ready to receive your feedback. Avoid giving feedback on the run, in a public place, or when the person you want to talk to is in the middle of other work. Don't, however, use this advice as a way of avoiding giving feedback at all!

- Feedback works best when it is mutual. If you notice that you are often giving feedback and not receiving it, ask for it. "I'd appreciate getting some feedback from you on how I handled that meeting in the mayor's office."
- The most helpful feedback consists of information that can be confirmed. If, for example, you tell me that my talking as much as I do leaves you feeling resentful because there is too little time left in meetings to hear what others have to say, I can check with others to see if they experience me in the same way.
- Give examples of the behavior if you are not delivering the feedback immediately after the incident. "Not only did you handle that police officer sensitively and firmly last week, but you also started a great conversation with the head of security when he looked uptight. When you create bridges like that, I feel confident that we have the leadership that we need in this organization." If you do not have specific examples (preferably more than one), it is better not to give feedback.
- Groups, teams, and whole organizations can quickly learn how and when to give feedback. Being asked to identify what made a meeting or a discussion effective or not effective helps people be descriptive and to notice what behaviors had what effect. Practicing the giving and receiving of feedback between individuals after meetings is a good way to internalize it within the life of an organization.

Over time, the practice of giving feedback reduces the likelihood that people will be judged in a public forum. If a group agrees that information about what is happening should, whenever possible, be given, the group will feel increasingly free to divulge their thoughts and feelings—and their trust level will rise.

Make It Legitimate to Get Third-Party Assistance

Most of us believe that people should be adult enough to deal with their conflicts in a mature way. Unfortunately, this belief is more of an expectation than a reality. Value differences, differences in style and personality, or different perspectives on issues affecting the life of the organization often will lead to polarizing confrontations rather than rational discussions where issues can be addressed. People often enter a discussion believing that the only persons who are going to change are their opponents. Few people approach such discussions with the thought that they might have to compromise or change their own positions.

Third-party mediation, either formal or informal, can make an enormous difference to an organization faced with internal conflict. A third party is simply an individual the opposing individuals or subgroups agree can play the role of mediator. This person talks to each side to discover their interests and to become aware of the emotional baggage which affects the conflict, and designs a process for dealing with the conflict. The role of the third party is that of facilitator, not judge; the objective is to lay out different points of view, to note the consequences of various behaviors on the organization, and to assist the people involved in getting beyond their positions to identifying their underlying interests or needs.[2]

Once the parties in conflict understand what each other's needs are, the facilitator assists them in brainstorming options to get past the win-lose character of the fight. When they develop a list of options, some will seem more appropriate than others for meeting a large part of their needs. Sometimes the parties need an additional step: to discuss criteria by which to evaluate the options that they brainstormed. When this much work has been done, an option usually emerges which provides each party with a compatible way forward.[3]

Members notice when conflicts are polarizing individuals or subgroups. If they request third-party mediation, there is a tendency for individuals to take more responsibility for solving their problem, even before a third party is brought into the situation. When this does not occur, leaders need to take initiative to make it happen.

Some organizations are building into their structure an agreement that, in cases of conflict which cannot be resolved by mediation, the parties must go to arbitration rather than take the issue to court. In arbitration, a third party acts as a judge, listening to all sides of the issue and then making a determination. This not only saves expenses and time, it also avoids the embarassment of "washing dirty linen" in public (sometimes to the delight of the opposition). New Society Publishers, for example, writes into the contract an author signs, a provision that arbitration be used instead of the courts, if disagreements cannot be resolved by mediation.

Sometimes a conflict is really as much about style and ego as about political and strategic differences. A third party may be able to help the people involved in the conflict to realize the impact of their different styles and personal issues. Some of this may be done in separate meetings with each party. When people come from different backgrounds it is important that the person chosen to be a third party be aware of how different cultures tend to handle conflict.

A variation of this approach is to set up, with an outside facilitator, a larger meeting specifically to deal with a conflict that affects the whole organization. Such a meeting can involve a substantial number and, with the skillful use of small groups, clear the air and get agreements for resolution.

Before leaving a meeting set up to resolve a conflict, the parties need to agree on a contract for how they will relate to each other in the future. A follow-up meeting might be scheduled to evaluate and to plan possible next steps.

It's hard to exaggerate what a difference it makes to grassroots and nonprofit groups when conflict resolution mechanisms become a regular part of their culture. Burnout declines, organizational challenges can be handled, and going to work brings joy even though social problems are still out there to be faced. Consistently using even a few of the suggestions in this chapter will strengthen your group.

Notes

1. For more on this dynamic and how to counter it, see Edwin H. Friedman, *Generation to Generation: Family Process in Church and Synagogue* (New York: Guildford, 1985).
2. For a handbook rich in detail for playing the role of mediator, see Christopher W. Moore, *The Mediation Process: Practical Strategies for Resolving Conflict* (San Francisco: Jossey-Bass, 1986).
3. Roger Fisher and William Ury, *Getting to Yes: Negotiating Agreements Without Giving In* (New York: Houghton-Mifflin, 1981).

Chapter 14

BALANCING DEMANDS OF THE JOURNEY

Using Negotiating Skills

DURING A RAFTING TRIP SOME PARTICIPANTS GET SO OCCUPIED WITH avoiding the next boulder that they forget where the trip is supposed to take them. Others keep their eyes so firmly glued to the horizon that they neglect to deal with immediate obstacles. For the raft to reach its goal, leaders must be able to balance the need for safety with the need for getting to the destination. They have to negotiate different perspectives and concerns.

Not only do leaders of democratic organizations need negotiating skills, so do the members. Knowing how to negotiate changes in the work environment adds to organizational effectiveness as well as personal satisfaction. Having the skills to negotiate changes in organizational strategy can prevent individuals and groups from becoming locked in power struggles that slow down progress toward organizational goals. In contrast, an organization where members expect their leaders to know and take care of their needs will breed powerlessness and resentment, and an organization where the most important objective is not to ruffle feathers will lose momentum and waste its creative potential. Without good negotiation skills, some groups find themselves overwhelmed by the needs of individuals, while others sacrifice individual needs to the group's mission.

Learning how to balance the many perspectives, approaches, and demands of organizational life means learning the art of negotiation. This chapter shares ideas about why and how to negotiate.

Develop Broad-Based Negotiating Skills in Your Organization

From an organizational point of view, broad-based negotiating skills increase democracy. For example, when staff or volunteers who differ can work out their disagreements on their own, managers need not step in and decide for them how things will be. Whether your organization functions as a hierarchy or a collective, well-distributed negotiating skills mean that decisions can benefit from different perspectives and take into account the needs both of the organization and of the people involved. Moreover, negotiated decisions are more likely to be implemented than those handed down by fiat, because people have had the opportunity to help shape them.

For you as an individual, being a skilled negotiator prevents frustration. You are more likely to influence the organization according to your best insights, and you are more likely to get what you need to do your work most effectively.

In a major national social change organization one department was eager to launch a boycott against an industrial giant. As the idea was being developed and other departments heard about it, doubts started to be voiced. Public relations doubted the media would pay enough attention to be effective; organizers in other departments doubted the availability of energy in the field. The advocates of the boycott heard about these doubts on the grapevine, and then talked among themselves to shore up their arguments. As the advocates researched boycotts and discussed the idea in their department, they became more and more certain they were right and the doubters were wrong. When cross-departmental encounters about the boycott did happen, the advocates and doubters talked past each other, with the advocates increasingly using a hard sell approach.

Finally the issue came to a head in an organization-wide meeting of all department heads, and the boycott was overwhelmingly rejected. The advocates were shaken and upset, and refused to give up; instead, they mobilized an emotional power struggle within the organization. The outcome was a substantially downscaled boycott which was adopted by the organization amidst demoralization and the departure of a key staffer.

—a consultant to the organization

Save Time and Stress by Initiating the Negotiating Process

We can all think of situations where hours and hours have gone into arguments and counterarguments, where power plays and hard sell have been used to influence the outcome of organizational decisions. Depending on our own position, we might also testify to the high cost of such a process, not just in terms of time and money, but also in terms of morale. The point of this chapter is that anyone advocating for a particular action would do well to initiate a negotiation process rather than a win/lose fight. Organizational leaders have a particular responsibility to see that this happens. When discussions are started before positions become rigid, a proposal is more likely to emerge that the whole organization can support. This, in turn, increases the likelihood of success.

What holds us back from initiating negotiation? Since successful negotiation requires listening, we may know intuitively that we do not want to listen, because we're right. Knowing we're right is a delicious feeling, but it often gets in the way of being effective. It reduces the feedback we need to hear if we are to grasp the situation more fully and communicate accurately and persuasively. When advocates have listened only to their own voices they often have trouble communicating with others and resort to a hard sell. This simply makes the opposition more entrenched. Step one in effective communication is quality listening.

Another block to initiating negotiation is our image of what negotiation is: we may equate negotiation with bargaining and believe that successful negotiation is a matter of hard bargainers winning over soft bargainers. The goal of the hard bargainer is victory; she or he typically digs into position, makes threats, misleads as to bottom line, applies pressure, and demands concessions as a condition of the relationship. The goal of the soft bargainer, on the other hand, is agreement; he or she typically changes position easily, makes offers instead of threats, discloses the bottom line, yields to pressure, and makes concessions in order to cultivate the relationship.

In *Getting to Yes*, a breakthrough book in this field, Roger Fisher and William Ury describe a more effective style of negotiating.[1] Fisher and Ury suggest changing the game by negotiating on the merits, even if the other party doesn't want to. In this third way, the goal is a wise outcome reached efficiently and amicably. The bargainer doesn't focus on his or her position, but instead on interests. Instead of making threats or offers, she or he explores interests; the bargainer avoids having a bottom line, refuses to yield to pressure, and doesn't link concessions to relationship. Instead, the principled bargainer separates the people from the problem and sees the bargaining process as an opportunity to invent options for mutual gain. This means that bargaining becomes a creative exercise rather than a contest of wills. In their book the authors suggest how to bargain in this style even when the other side wants to do the old fashioned power struggle.

Take a Step Back from the Conflict in Order to See What's Really Possible

When we negotiate many of us can't see the forest for the trees. We may start out knowing the goal we want to achieve, but quickly loose track of solving the problem as we focus on competing with the other side. Soon, instead of wanting to win people over to support our objectives, we want to win over people. Not a great way to build an organization! As Fisher and Ury describe in their book, separating the people from the problem can make a world of difference here. It also helps to learn how to separate people's interests from their positions. The following fictionalized example illustrates what these principles mean:

> *Trudy and Fernando went to the executive committee meeting excited about what they'd just discovered: the governor was coming to the biggest downtown hotel next week to lunch with business leaders about economic development plans. What a chance to crash the party and demand a major program of affordable housing for the homeless! A small group could go in, refuse to leave, get arrested, refuse bail, and fast for a week. That way, they figured, there could be news stories day after day. When they came to the executive committee meeting they were disappointed to see only three others there—bad weather was keeping half the committee home.*
>
> *Alan also arrived at the meeting with high anticipation. He had just persuaded Naimah, the group's chairperson, that the highest priority for the group was developing a strategic plan instead of*

191

"lurching from action to action."

The fight was predictable. "How can you give up a chance like this to get in the governor's face in order to think about next year and the year after? We may not even be here next year, this city's falling apart so fast!" "Our organization is losing credibility with funders and even our volunteers because we have no game plan, we just react all the time. It burns us out without getting us anywhere!"

Gloria, who was one of the group's founders and still functioned on the board, although in a less active role, intervened. "I know what Trudy and Fernando want us to do now, and I also know what position Alan and Naimah are taking. What I'd like to know more about is what the four of you think the organization needs and what you need. Like, what are the bigger goals that you have for developing the organization to be more effective in taking on homelessness? A big picture may help all of us figure out what we can agree to."

After some hestitation, they created lists of goals, which included "militancy," "high public profile," "specific concrete victories," "more financial resources," "more influence with elected officials," and "less turnover among volunteers."

"Those are great lists," Gloria said, "and some of us might have questions to ask about some of them." The group clarified a few of them, but most were obvious. "Now how about we start coming up with ways we can meet some of the interests of both? Like, what are some options—let's just brainstorm and later we can figure out what might work."

The group brainstormed a series of options and had a probing discussion comparing them, complete with one more emotional flare-up. As they learned more about each others' priority interests, agreement began to take shape around one of the options: to go all out on the governor's lunch, followed by a three month internal campaign to create a long-range strategic plan.

"One reason this agreement seems so solid to me," Gloria remarked as she summed up, "is that we're going to do for ourselves exactly what we're demanding that the governor do: create a real plan that mobilizes resources effectively." The group laughed appreciatively and agreed on who would talk with the absent committee members.

Consider Creating an Organizational Caucus to Make Effective Negotiations More Possible

One reason many people fear caucuses is that they are considered divisive. Keeping that danger in mind, there are nevertheless times when a point of view is not taken seriously and needs to be supported by a caucus in order to make negotiations possible. Whether a caucus is divisive or contributes toward overall unity depends on whether it is secretive or open. If it is open, its existence is a statement of what is true in the organization (that is, that a certain point of view is held by a subgroup), and organizations need the truth in order to develop and grow stronger. If it is secretive, a caucus may seriously undermine organizational cohesion.

In response to growing strains in a large national social change organization, a group of staff and volunteers decided to organize a radical caucus which they called, after British tradition, a "ginger group." Their purpose was to develop a proposal for a major, innovative program that was a dramatic departure from the way the organization had been operating and would have strong implications organization-wide.

The group told the executive director about its existence and that its meetings were open to all who wanted to participate, and negotiated a regular meeting place inside the organizational headquarters. The result was a substantial lessening of fear about what the group might be thinking and greater receptivity to the proposal when it was issued.

—a member of the caucus, who had been active in the organization for many years

---

Some caucuses begin as informal networks of members of oppressed groups—African Americans, for example, or gays—and later become a formally recognized part of the organizational structure. The American Friends Service Committee, for example, has a staffed office at its headquarters serving the interests of people of color among staff and volunteers.[2]

Make Use of Your Growing Negotiation Skills in Building Coalitions

Within an organization, lack of negotiating skill is sometimes remedied by managerial decisions from above or the board acting as a final arbiter when staff and volunteers cannot reach agreement. The structure of most coalitions of organizations, however, leaves no higher authority to settle disputes and no compelling interest that forces the differing sides to work out their differences. Therefore, acute conflicts put the coalition itself at risk if the participants don't make use of negotiation as a means to develop positions and approaches that will meet the various needs of the coalition partners. In this way, developing negotiating skills within a group can be beneficial in achieving the group's goals that require work with coalitions.

The Vietnam war hit U.S. society hard, and by the mid-1960s more and more disparate groups started to oppose it. The groups varied greatly by ideology, race, culture, and strategy. Putting together an anti-war coalition was a challenging task, and keeping it together nearly impossible. The nearly impossible was made possible, until he died, by the coalition chair, A.J. Muste. A.J. was an octogenarian pacifist who kept the respect of advocates of armed struggle and of students whose slogan was "Never trust anyone over thirty." One thing going for him was a reputation of massive integrity earned in struggles for justice dating to the Lawrence textile strike of 1919. Perhaps more important was his standard operating procedure: find out ahead of the meeting what the points of view are, and negotiate, negotiate, negotiate!

Notes

1. Roger Fisher and William Ury, *Getting to Yes: Negotiating Agreements Without Giving In* (New York: Houghton-Mifflin, 1981) p. 13.
2. Psychologist and organizational consultant Arnold Mindell has developed an approach to leadership which he calls "deep democracy," through which minority voices are empowered to negotiate solutions that benefit the whole organization. See, for example, his book *Leadership as a Martial Art: Techniques and Strategies for Resolving Conflict and Creating Community* (San Francisco: HarperSan Francisco, 1992). For a helpful summary of studies which see organizations as political systems, therefore involving negotiation of interests, see Gareth Morgan's landmark book, *Images of Organization* (Newbury Park, Calif.: Sage, 1986).

194

Chapter 15

PACING YOURSELF FOR THE JOURNEY

How to Avoid Burnout and Thrive while Working to Change the World

S TRESS COMES WITH THE TERRITORY OF WORKING FOR SOCIAL CHANGE. IT'S not all bad. The right amount of stress feels stimulating or like a challenging lifestyle. With too much stress, on the other hand, we risk burnout. One common cause for burnout is a malfunctioning organization. Since most of this book focuses on shaping up organizational structure and function, the major part of this last chapter is directed to individuals. A more relaxed you will be an important first step in repairing or improving your organization.

Some of us function year after year with too much stress. We may find ourselves being relatively unhappy and unfulfilled, judgmental of others, overeating, losing weight, or developing addictive behaviors. We may handle conflict poorly by avoiding it, being defensive or aggressive, or allowing unresolved conflicts to disrupt our work.

In this chapter you won't learn a quick fix for chronic overwork. Just as we don't expect social transformation from a few demonstrations, we can't expect to discover our optimal challenge level through a couple of tricks. Instead we encourage looking at the big picture of your life and building a holistic strategy for change with the techniques that work for you.

Don't Let Work Take Over

Review a typical month in your datebook and notice what it says about balance: How many evenings and weekends did you work without taking off compensatory time to do other things that renew and refresh you? Move toward balancing your activism with something else that reminds you how good it is to be alive. If you draw all your social life from your work situation or your volunteer work, consider making new friends based on hobbies or recreation. This also relieves the tunnel vision which activists can get from hanging out only with each other.

Overwork often has the effect of reinforcing low self-esteem. When we choose to work too long, we are in effect telling ourselves we aren't worthy unless we do that. We also leave family members, friends, and lovers feeling undervalued and unappreciated. They may have trouble objecting because, after all, the cause is obviously more important than they are. We get a cycle of unworthiness.

The fundament of our work is that we as black women are tremendously oppressed in many ways and a large part of that oppression has been internalized and we act it out on ourselves even if there isn't an active external oppression. So, within the Black Women's Health Project we are faithful to the principle that women need to heal themselves and so we never do work without play. We just finished doing a conference in Barbados and the first three days in Barbados we spent at their local carnival. That was no accident. We made sure that we had three days of play before we got into the work. After my staff works real hard I hire a masseuse for them so that they can get full body massages. We did an organizing conference that was futile so afterward we treated ourselves to a cruise.

—African American leader who was formerly a staff member of the project

Break the cycle by taking vacations—long, short, spontaneous, planned, alone, together. A little rest and recreation can go a long way toward dispelling fatigue and burnout. Hard to schedule and justify a good vacation in the middle of the crises that continually pop up? Think of it this way: if you had an accident and were disabled for two weeks, the job would certainly survive your absence. If you suddenly had an attack of the flu and were bedridden for a week, the job would survive.

If you are genuinely indispensable to the daily work of your organization, then your organization may not be very healthy. Even if you think that you are indispensable, try planning a vacation well ahead of time, publicizing it so that everyone expects you to be gone and letting them know how critical tasks will be taken care of in your absence.

A spontaneous day or two off can be terrific, and those around you may be relieved to find you returning with more energy and a renewed sense of humor. Why wait until you are sick to take a day off—take the day when you can enjoy it, and you may not need to get sick.

Most activists say they don't have time to read, yet reading is one of the simplest ways of getting away from the stress of our work. "I take time every day to trash my mind, to take myself away from what it is that bothers me, and fill my mind instead with a good mystery or story," says one experienced activist. "I find I can't do this at night because I fall asleep, so I personally cut a little bit of time from work every day and make it a regular part of my diet."

Physical fitness pays off in every area of your life including the amount of stress you can gracefully carry. That means sleep enough for you (different people need different amounts), eat well and regularly, and exercise.

One grassroots leader says that three times a week (two times at lunch and once at 3:30 on Thursdays) he plays racquetball at the local Y. Everyone at the office knows and expects this routine. It is built in as a disciplined part of his life. "I simply never think of work when I'm hitting a ball at sixty miles an hour in a small, four-walled court." He sees social, emotional, and physical benefits to this routine, which takes three hours out of a typical sixty- to seventy-hour week. Others in the office appreciate that he does this for himself, because they see the benefits for him and for themselves.

—consultant to the organization

Don't go it alone. Psychologist Stephanie Simonton, in reviewing the research on the relation of stress to cancer, says that the more individuals from whom we draw intimate support, the more stress we can handle well. Family members, lovers, and close friends provide important support, but depending only on these sources runs the risk of overloading them. A romantic relationship, for example, can wear out under continual use for work-related support.

> *A board member of one social action group made an unusual offer to the executive director: "I have peer counseling skills and want to make part of my volunteer board work giving you a listening ear once a week." The director took her up on it, and for several years spent a half hour once a week, on his way to work, using her quality attention to "think out loud" about the job. What he said was totally in confidence. He could talk, complain, be angry, and even express his fears and sadness. He found this chance to vent his feelings in a safe place gave him more clarity and strength in leading the staff.*
>
> —a consultant to the organization

Consider starting a support group. The group might start with a core of three and extend to as many as eight. Regular attendance and regularly scheduled meetings make a strong support group. The key is a mutual willingness by the members to be open and candid about the critical issues that affect their lives. Usually the group begins with work- or cause-related problems; when trust grows, personal issues may also show up because of the close relationship between the personal and the political. A support group can be fairly informal, but will require some regularity and agreement on how it will operate.[1]

In our society women usually find it easier to maintain support groups than men, who traditionally don't share feelings, inadequacies, and vulnerabilities with each other. Men starting a support group may need to give it extra attention to compensate for this difficulty, which comes with men's socialization. Look for local resources: there may be a sympathetic professional or someone with experience in the men's antisexist movement who could facilitate initial meetings or be a resource in some other way.

From the Quaker tradition comes a means of providing structured feedback for activists: the clearness committee. A person who wants this support asks three to seven people she or he trusts to come together to help sort out difficult issues or directions for the future. People who are asked to participate generally have different points of view and a variety of experiences, so the group represents as wide a range of perspectives as possible. A clearness session of several hours enables the focus person to receive supportive and critical feedback which leaves her or him in much better shape to solve a problem or make a decision about next steps in their activist work.[2]

Leaders in particular have a tendency to feel isolated. A support group for leaders can make a difference, providing an opportunity for solving mutual problems or getting feedback and guidance on individual issues. Often our judgment is hampered by the lack of input from others we respect, and to whom we have little normal access. One barrier to leader support groups is that leaders often like to appear as though they have everything under control and don't need help. Another barrier to leaders from related organizations being in the same support group is the competition that may exist between their organizations.

A great leader is an individual who can generate the most choices concerning a given problem or situation, and has the wisdom to see the difference between them. A support group can generate more choices, and therefore support the greatness of each of the persons within it. This is good enough reason to surmount the barriers and create a support group, not to mention the stress reduction inherent in the comradeship of the group.

Define Attainable Goals

One way to increase stress is to have vague and far-reaching goals for your work: "peace," "liberation," "ecological balance," etc. You then can never do enough to deserve a rest, a slower pace. Create goals that are attainable, not only for the organization, but for you in the organization. The goals can be tough and demanding, just make them achievable.

If you do choose a goal that is a real stretch for you—say, fundraising to increase the budget by twenty-five percent in a year—then it pays to set a goal in your personal life which is easily achieved, like making your bed every day or flossing your teeth. Making progress on your personal goal builds confidence so it is less stressful to reach for your work goal.

> *I've done a lot of projects in my 30+ years, and I choose them very carefully. I look around to see what isn't getting a lot of attention—maybe an issue that's neglected, or a method of work the movement isn't developing very well, for example cross-class organizing. There are a lot of gaps at any given time, so I have lots of choices! Then I ask myself what I would find personally challenging and would get a kick out of taking on. That narrows down the choices. Then I think about what is doable in terms of fundraising, location, other people to work with closely. (Sometimes I go to conferences to check people out that I might be working with, to see if I could get along with them with mutual respect.)*
>
> *Toward the end of the process something 'clicks' and I know what I want to do next. I realize other activists have other ways of going about making choices, which is fine. What I like about my way is that I always know why I'm doing what I'm doing—when the going gets tough— and how I personally am growing through it even if the project is floundering. So I never think of myself as a martyr, even if other people think I live a sacrificing type of life. Really, I love to do activism this way. My projects always connect with my heart.*
>
> —a veteran working-class activist

Find a Balance of Competence and Challenge

One way people burn themselves out is to take on tasks that are too easy or too hard for them. In the first case, people get bored; in the second, they get overwhelmed. What works best is finding a balance between areas of mastery and areas of challenge.[3]

Balance is an individual question. Some people enjoy work that has relatively little challenge; others enjoy work that pushes beyond their limits. In order to find the right balance for your group, feel free to shake up the existing distribution of responsibilities. If leaders have trouble delegating, push them to delegate. If someone is sinking under the weight of too many difficult tasks, shift the tasks around. Don't be rigid about job descriptions; remember that people are most productive when they have the right balance of competence and stretch.

What if you want to take on a task which may overwhelm you? Train for it. Go to workshops, call in a consultant, or get coaching from someone in your constituency who has those fundraising skills, that computer expertise, that mass media polish, or whatever you are wanting. Training can be the most efficient way to increase your competency, and therefore reduce your stress.

Don't let your concern for political correctness get in the way of learning and gaining resources. Someone with the expertise you want may also have attitudes or behaviors that you don't like or agree with. Keep perspective: life is not about perfection, it is about learning and growing. If you show that you know how to use available resources to learn and grow, others may follow your example.

Another training technique is to visit an expert. One activist spent two weeks as a shadow-intern to a chief executive officer who was known as an efficient, well-organized manager. The experience proved to be invaluable and gave the individual a handful of much needed tools for operating her organization. An AIDS activist spent a week in another state with a program director who was an excellent coalition builder. An additional advantage of such visits is that they build networks that are useful in a variety of ways over time.

Increase Structure, Supervision, and Feedback

Because changing society is a never-ending struggle, it's easy to be confused about when you are doing enough. A source of stress, therefore, is insufficient feedback, inadequate supervision, not having a structure which gives us permission to go home with the feeling of a job well done. Too often we are left to our own, often biased, perceptions of how we are doing, and so we are limited in how we can grow and change.

Structures can reduce anxiety. Supervision can make sure people get the feedback they deserve for their work, so they can watch themselves grow over time and become more effective. Volunteers, staff, and leaders all need accountability structures and feedback.

A feedback system which works well in activist groups is estimation/self-estimation. The focus person presents to the group her or his view of strengths and areas where his or her work needs improvement. Then the group responds, commenting both on what the focus person said and also pointing out strengths and areas of growth which were not mentioned in the presentation. Usually the group also thinks about what kind of support is needed in order to grow in those areas.

This method can be used by everyone in turn, including the director. Estimation/self-estimation reduces stress, because in a supportive atmosphere people can find out how others see them and their work rather than wonder and worry.[4]

Delegate, Delegate, Delegate!

Whether you are an executive director or a field organizer, the board chair or a volunteer fundraiser, there is almost certainly more to delegate than is your current practice. The pressures not to delegate are probably linked to what is burning you out—like perfectionism, distrust of others, feeling isolated, and not knowing other people who would like to participate in the project. Deciding to delegate is one sure way to discover and confront what pulls you down. Even the smallest steps of delegation are steps toward your own well-being. Realize that delegation is a win-win: a leader who does not effectively delegate tasks (and follow up on their status) smothers the growth of staff and volunteers, stifles their creativity and initiative, and contributes to program bottlenecks.

If you think: "But they don't know how to do this well," then remember that empowerment means expecting things to take longer when people are learning and that it is a fine use of time. Support the learner through training sessions and a mentoring program. If you feel impatient that it takes the time it takes, that impatience is another internal pressure for you to confront and work through in order to be effective for the long run in working for your cause.

In short, go on a campaign to delegate your work, and welcome the obstacles that get in your way; the obstacles have their own juicy potential for your empowerment and the effectiveness of the organization.

Enjoy the Work and Have Fun

Humor may be necessary for survival; consider the rich traditions of humor among African Americans, Jews, gays, and other survivors. Take a chance on being bizarre or corny. The worst that will happen is that you're the only one laughing—and that's one more than was laughing before. According to psychologist David Abramis, bringing fun into the office increases creativity and productivity.[5]

Activists commonly have "To Do" lists they carry around. Here's an idea: add a "To Be" heading, and when you write your list of tasks, also write how you want to be while you do your tasks.

People thrive on ritual, celebration, and play. Singing and storytelling has been a hallmark of the black freedom movement and other groups as well. Some groups build playful ritual right into their meetings. One way is starting a meeting with "news and goods," in which each person briefly tells of something good that happened for them in the past week or two. Some of the anecdotes are bound to be funny, and the atmosphere lightens up immediately. Another quick way to lighten up meetings is to play brief games, sometimes called "Light 'n' Livelies." A couple people usually groan at the thought ("How corny!"), and a few minutes later smiles appear and energy returns.[6]

> **In the Piedmont Peace Project much of the organizing is itself celebratory: in a voter registration drive, admission to a big picnic is your voter registration form. The Project has a choir, which means lots of music and special celebrations as well as building the Project. Look for opportunities to give awards, recognition.**
>
> —*a leader in the project*

The potluck is a ritual feature of many groups. Celebrations are opportunities for affirmations and appreciation, and can be seen as rewards for holding on to and pursuing the right values in a society which is still oppressive. One organization we know holds numerous fundraising dance parties: they don't always raise much money, but the members love to dance.

Fortunately, resources for ritual and celebration are increasing.

203

Along with play they ease stress because they speak deeply to our need for community and for release.[7]

> *My first time in jail was during a civil rights campaign in a small industrial city where race relations were really terrible. There was a lot of police violence against us, and I was scared to be sent to the county prison where it seemed they'd have us at their mercy. I was completely surprised by the attitude of our movement folks. Instead of being tense and depressed, our group was active and full of spirit. We marched together up and down the cell block lustily singing movement songs, and most anytime except "lights out" there'd be some of us singing or telling stories*
>
> — a European American activist

Use Time Well

The sense of scarcity about time is a huge source of stress for all of us living in a modern industrial society. It can be a source of tension in some groups, between those who have combined their social world with their cause work, on the one hand, and those who have families and friends outside the group. The first group may prolong a meeting by cracking jokes or sharing rumors, while the second group is restless because the children are waiting at home, a lover wants some attention, or they want to curl up and finish their mystery novel.

Time management techniques reduce stress in an organization as does the methodology for running more effective meetings.

Face and Resolve Conflicts

Psychiatrist and writer M. Scott Peck believes that the single greatest cause of mental illness in our society is our unwillingness to deal with the conflicts in our own lives—we avoid, deny, procrastinate, and hope that the conflicts will resolve themselves.[8] When we do that we are in effect telling ourselves that we can't cope, so we're lowering our self-esteem and increasing our stress. In the chapter on conflict resolution you'll find some useful tools. No tools will help if you aren't willing to summon your courage and deal with the conflicts around you.

204

One reason not to deal with conflicts outside is because they relate to conflicts inside. All of us have internal conflicts; ironically, the more we deny them, the more influence they are likely to have unconsciously and the more risk we run of burnout. Fortunately, there are ways of working with our internal conflicts which increase our effectiveness. The first step is being willing to acknowledge a conflict to ourselves, and the second is being willing not to condemn one of the parts of us which seems to be at war with another part, but instead to take a compassionate and responsible attitude toward ourself in the situation.[9]

Relax!

We generally do our best work when we are in a state of relaxed alertness. Here are some specific tools which many find helpful for relaxing in the midst of tension. Bookstores have books on these topics with more details. These brief descriptions are here to intrigue you and get you started.

Meditation.

The daily use of meditation for fifteen to twenty minutes provides a greater sense of well-being, inner peace and personal confidence. During meditation, and for some time after, people are measurably more relaxed. All you need is yourself and a quiet place. While meditation is a skill that can be highly developed over time, its benefits are almost immediate even for the novice. It helps to meditate at the same time each day, if possible, to become a part of your routine. The best time depends on your lifestyle, but after eating is not a good idea unless you really would rather nap.

Self-hypnosis.

Like meditation, it can be a practical tool for almost everyone, with a variety of uses in addition to reducing stress. When you hypnotize yourself you can regain self-control after a tense situation; say, after being in a heated argument. Your muscles relax, your breathing deepens, your pulse slows down, and anxiety subsides. This is a great way to get ready for a high-pressure negotiation session, or a fundraising pitch where the stakes are high.

Reflective Imaging.

Remember a place in your life that represents peace and tranquility? The human mind is capable of recreating such images and generating the feelings that go with them. First, take several minutes to breathe deeply and tighten then release the muscle groups. At the end of that time, shut your eyes and recreate in your mind a picture of this favorite, quiet place. Some people experience the place not so much as a picture, but as a set of sounds, smells, or sensations. When you do this repeatedly you will find the place becomes more vivid and you can flow into it more easily. The heartbeat slows, the breathing deepens, and you relax.

Let Go of Guilt, Resentment and Fear

One source of stress is inside you: the guilt, fear, and resentment which may be part of your motivation for justice and a better world. It's natural to have those feelings, and they often get us started as activists. The trouble is, guilt, fear, and resentment become a burden in the long run and a drain on creativity and hope. We're distinguishing between anger and resentment: when anger is expressed promptly and appropriately, it can be cleansing and powerful. Resentment is suppressed anger and hurts the person who holds it most of all.

When people are driven by guilt, accomplishments and small successes are never enough and leave them with a gnawing sense of failure or inadequacy. When guilt motivates us, there is never enough time, our efforts are never good enough, and we're likely to get into comparison games with others over who is working the hardest or has suffered the most (and gets burned out the quickest!). Guilt also pushes us to prove our worthiness by working for justice. We may find ourselves unable to set clear boundaries between work and other parts of our lives. Our refusal to care for ourselves makes it hard for others to see our vision of a caring society.

Fortunately, only a part of our motivation for change comes from distress. "A true revolutionary," as guerrilla leader Che Guevara reportedly said, "is guided by feelings of great love." A part of our work is standing up for ourselves, acknowledging that we are worthy and deserving of a just society, and asserting that love is in our hearts. How can we grow away from the negative emotions which stress us, and toward the positive motivation of worthiness and caring?

Keeping a journal, the consistent writing down of thoughts, feelings, and ideas, can reduce stress by getting feelings out, providing a tracking system for growth, and providing distance and perspective on the conflicts and pressures around us. Honest journaling is a source of continuing education and growth as you express the crucial issues that you face, as spontaneously as possible.

Therapy has assisted numerous people to stay in the struggle by making internal changes in attitude and external changes in behavior. Therapy can be expensive, but some therapists charge on a sliding scale according to ability to pay, and can also be asked to reduce their charge as a contribution to the cause for which you are working. Personal growth seminars have developed powerful ways of assisting people to work from a more centered, positive place.[10]

A peer counseling method used by some activists is Re-evaluation Counseling, also called "co-counseling." Re-evaluation Counseling enables people to free themselves of accumulated distress experiences (such as fear, hurt, and loss) that begin early in life. The method entails two people taking turns counseling and being counseled. The person acting as counselor mostly listens and draws the other out. The person acting as client talks and discharges emotions connected with present problems or old memories in physical ways, such as laughing and crying. With experience and increased confidence, the process helps new perspectives to emerge as old feelings begin to lose their power.[11]

Other ways of nurturing our positive motivation, and thereby reducing stress, include prayer (especially thankfulness and praise), reading inspiring biographies, reading and writing poetry, and, as described above, getting the support of a buddy or an activist support group.

Create a Vision for Your Life

The most effective people tend to have dreams, plans, and visions of the future. Some idea of where they are going promotes a sense of hope and well-being in their lives and provides something to shoot for beyond the here and now. Having such a vision or dream helps maintain a clear and balanced perspective on the present.

Notes

1. For practical information on how support groups can assist in bringing balance and integrity to the lives of people working for social justice, see the manual *Insight and Action* by Tova Green, Peter Woodrow, and Fran Peavey (Philadelphia and Gabriola Island, B.C.: New Society Publishers, 1994).
2. Ibid.
3. This is similar to the point of view in Anne Herbert's article, "Let the Good Times Last," *Whole Earth Review*, March 1985, pp. 65–74.
4. Virginia Coover, et al, *Resource Manual for a Living Revolution* (Philadelphia and Gabriola Island, B.C.: New Society Publishers, 1977).
5. David Abramis, "Work Smarter, Not Harder," *Psychology Today* (NEXG 1989), pp. 33–38.
6. The new games movement has produced many books of games which are fun, energy-boosting, and inclusive. A manual which includes a number of games which are brief enough to use in indoor meetings, "For the Fun of It!," is included in Stephanie Judson, ed., *A Manual on Nonviolence and Children* (Philadelphia and Gabriola Island, B.C. New Society Publishers, 1984)); two of the authors routinely use these with adults in our consulting practice.
7. Groups for prayer, guided meditation, and various forms of worship are available in most places. Drumming is growing in the men's movement. Full moon and other rituals developed by women who practice wicce are flourishing. See Starhawk *The Spiral Dance* for a a rich array of rituals in this tradition (San Francisco: Harper and Row, 1979). Singing and dancing have provided emotional release over the centuries.
8. In his book *The Road Less Travelled* (New York: Touchstone Books, 1988), M. Scott Peck vividly discusses denial and practical ways of inner change which makes handling conflicts easier.
9. Outlining internal conflict resolution strategies is beyond the scope of this book, but the interested reader can find an abundance of resources. See, for example, consultant Elaine Yarbrough, "Making Peace with Yourself," in Neil Wollman, ed., *Working for Peace: A Handbook of Practical Psychology and Other Tools* (San Luis Obispo, Calif.: Impact Publishers, 1985), pp. 55–62. One frequent arena for inner conflict is money; the Impact Project was organized by activists to assist people to work through their money issues. See their annotated bibliography and resource list, "Taking Charge of our Money, our Values, and our Lives." (The Impact Project, 21 Linwood St., Arlington, MA 02174).
10. Insight Seminars and Lifespring are two highly competent seminars which are based on humanistic psychology. An organization responsible for much of what we know about group dynamics, human relations training, and self-development is NTL Institute in Alexandria, Va.
11. For information contact Re-evaluation Counseling Communities, 719 Second Ave. N, Seattle, Washington 98109.

EPILOGUE

THE RIVER METAPHOR IN THIS BOOK IMPLIES A COURSE THAT IS SOMETIMES calm but often turbulent, and focuses on the understandings, structures, and skills necessary for navigating through white water as well as getting out of the backwaters. We recommend that leaders committed to working for a better world help their organizations develop a long term perspective, a vision of where they are headed as well as what it will take to get there. We hope that the suggestions and the experiences shared in these pages will provide useful guidance through uncertain waters. We invite you to take a fresh look at the obstacles and opportunities facing you and your organization. Try some of the ideas that have worked in other settings or adapt them to your own circumstances.

We cannot know the future but we can be certain that it will demand organizational flexibility and creativity as well as personal maturity, strength, and courage. It will demand leaders that can keep their eyes on the goal while at the same time supporting the crew in avoiding the boulders that block the way, making necessary course corrections and keeping the raft in good repair.

This book started with a discussion of social change movements and ended by focusing on the needs of involved individuals. The organization is the vehicle through which individuals together can make a difference. To succeed a leader focuses simultaneously on the social context, the individual participants and the organization as a whole.

This book is about creating organizations that support the growth of individual women and men while working to change the world. It is about doing good work in ways that help us thrive and have fun, as we take our place in what Dr. King called "the beloved community."

INDEX

Abramis, David, 203
Accountability
    of Board of Directors, 89–
        91, 93
    of supervisors, 142–143
ACTUP, 39, 46n15
Agenda, meeting
    development of, 119–123
AIDS, 7, 39
American Friends Service
    Committee, 6, 193
American Indian move-
    ment, 24
Amnesty International, 32
Anti-Vietnam War move-
    ment, 24, 25, 146, 194
    leadership in, 31
Authority
    of Board of Directors, 92–
        94
    and influence compared,
        95
    limits of, 96–101

Board of Directors, 70, 72–
    74, 81
    accountability of, 89–91
    authority of, 92–94
    meetings of, 87–88
    membership of, 85–87

orientation and training
    of, 91–92
responsibilities of, 82–85
size of, 88–89
Bobo, Kim, 35
Body politic, the
    MAP and, 17
Boulding, Elise, 9
Brainstorming
    use of, in meetings, 122
Burdet, Michele, 156n1
Bylaws, 83
    role of, in organizational
        structure, 66

Campaigning, social
    change
    manuals for, 12n3
    use of nonviolent action
        in, 40–41
Capitalism, 8
    unemployment and, 14
Capra, Fritjof, 79, 103
Caucus, organizational
    as negotiation tool, 193
CEO. See Chief executive
    officer
Chalice and the Blade,
    The (Eisler), 79
Chaos level
    of community building, 43

Chaos theory, 3
Charitable status
    of nonprofit corporations,
        78–79
Chavez, Cesar, 7, 40, 46–
    47n16
Chief executive officer
    (CEO), 82
Chief operating officer
    (COO), 82
Civil disobedience, 7, 46–
    47n16
Civil rights movement, 7
    funding and, 37–38
    morale building in, 149
    and stage eight of MAP,
        24
    and stage four of MAP, 20
Clearness committee
    as means of coping with
        stress, 199
Clergy
    leadership of, in civil
        rights movement, 7
Coaching
    and leadership, 99, 100
Co-counseling. See Re-
    evaluation Counseling
Collective
    as form of organizational
        structure, 75–76

Communication, 177–178
    negotiation and, 190
    See also Feedback; Listening, active
Communism, 8
    influence of, on social movements, 7
    Solidarity and, 34
Community-building, levels of, 42–44
Competence
    role of, in coping with stress, 201
    role of, in trust-building, 175, 176
Conflict resolution, 173–175
    as means of coping with stress, 204–205
    role of active listening in, 178–182
    role of communication norms in, 176–178
    role of feedback in, 183–185
    role of third-party mediation in, 185–187
    role of trust-building in, 175–176
COO. *See* Chief operating officer
Cooptation, fear of, 37
Council model
    as form of organizational structure, 74
Criticism, and feedback compared, 183

Decision-making structure and authority, 100–101
Delegation
    as means of coping with stress, 202

Development, organizational
    of diversity, 158–160, 168–171
    and improving morale, 155–156
    use of steering committee for, 104
Different Drum, The (Peck), 43
Direct action, power of, 39
Diversity, 11, 24, 165–166
    organizational assessment of, 161–163
    organizational development of, 158–160, 168–171
    recruitment for, 163–164
    use of identity groups in developing, 167–168
Dolci, Danilo, 33
Domination, 30
    power-over and, 28–29
Door-knocking
    use of, in neighborhood organizing, 51–52
Duty of care, 85
Duty of loyalty, 85
Duty of obedience, 85

Economic reorganization
    influence of, on social movements, 7
Education
    MAP and, 19, 22
Educational status
    of nonprofit corporations, 78–79
Eisler, Riane, 29–30, 79
Emotional dynamics
    in meetings, 125–126
Empowerment, 15
    problem-solving and, 34–35

supervision and, 131
Environmentalists
    use of nonviolent action by, 41
Estimation/self-estimation
    as form of evaluation, 149–151, 201–202
Evaluation, 201–202
    group morale and, 149–151
    of meetings, 126–128
    of supervisors, 138–141
    See also Feedback
Executive Director
    as element of organizational structure, 70–74

Facilitation, 10–11
    importance of, in meetings, 123–125
Farmworkers union, 24.
    See also United Farmworkers
Feedback, 114–116, 149–151
    failure as, 53–54
    and organizational structure, 67
    role of, in conflict resolution, 183–185
    role of, in coping with stress, 201–202
    for supervisors, 135–137
    See also Evaluation; Information gathering
Fee structures, 83
Fisher, Roger, 190, 191
Freeman, Jo, 75
Funding, 37–38, 90
    scarcity mentality and, 86, 87

Gandhi, Mahatma
    use of nonviolent action by, 41

Getting to Yes: Negotiating Agreements Without Giving In (Fisher and Ury), 190–191
Goals, organizational
　defining of, 199–200
Gossip
　role of, in conflict resolution, 182
Grassroots movement
　and stage four of MAP, 20
Growth
　of activist organizations, 58–63
Guevera, Che, 206

Harding, Vincent, 3
Hierarchy
　as form of organizational structure, 70, 71–74
Humor
　as means of coping with stress, 203

Identity groups, 9
　building diversity through, 167–168
Incorporation
　articles of, 83
　structural organization and, 76–79
Influence, and authority compared, 95
Information gathering
　organizational planning and, 113–116
Intervention, third-party
　as form of nonviolent action, 41
Intimacy
　role of, in trust-building, 175
IRS. *See* U.S. Internal Revenue Service

"I statements"
　role of, in feedback, 184

Jesus, 7
Job descriptions
　supervision and, 133
Jobs with Peace
　use of house meetings by, 52
Johnson, Lyndon, 38

Kendall, Jackie, 35
King, Martin Luther, Jr., 17, 38, 44

Labor, division of
　in meetings, 123–125
Lakey, George, 40
Leadership
　authority and, 95, 96–101
　information gathering and, 114–116
　in primary system, 59
　in social movements, 30–32, 34
　support for, 199
Legal advice, 84
Listening, active
　role of, in conflict resolution, 178–182

Macy, Joanna, 33
Malcolm X, 152
Management, 10
　as element of organizational structure, 71–74
Manual for Direct Action, A (Oppenheimer and Lakey), 40
MAP. *See* Movement Action Plan
Marcos, Ferdinand, 30
Martyr syndrome

　and morale building, 153–154
Marxism, 9
Max, Steve, 35
Media
　effect of, on morale, 145–146
　narrowness of view of, 156n1
Mediation, third-party
　role of, in conflict resolution, 185–187
Meditation
　as means of coping with stress, 205
Meetings, 87–88, 118
　dealing with emotional dynamics in, 125–126
　developing an agenda for, 119–123
　division of labor in, 123–125
　evaluation of, 126–128
　facilitation of, 10–11
　and limits of authority, 100
Meetings, group
　in primary system, 59
Meetings, house
　use of, in neighborhood organizing, 52
Membership
　of Board of Directors, 85–87
　organizational structure and, 65–67
Milk, Harvey, 51
Mission, clarification of, 36
Mission statement
　and organizational planning, 107–109
Mobilizing
　manuals for, 12n3
Money. *See* Funding

Morale, 11
  and confronting internal-
    ized oppression, 151–152
  effect of media on, 145–146
  importance of, 144
  organizational develop-
    ment and, 155–156
  and personal *vs.* political,
    153–155
  and self-respect, 147–151
Morris, Aldon D., 12n5
Movement Action Plan
    (MAP), 26n4, 112
  stages of, 17–25
Moyers, Bill, 26n4, 112
  and MAP, 17–25, 145
Muste, A. J., 194

NAFTA. See North Ameri-
    can Free Trade Agree-
    ment
Name-calling
  as obstacle to diversity,
    165–166
Napier, Rod, 101, 130n
National Organization for
    Women, 32
National Public Radio, 49
Negotiation skills
  organizational need for,
    188–194
New games movement,
    208n6
New Society Publishers
  mission statement of, 108
  use of arbitration by, 186
New Yorker, The, 49
Nixon, Richard
  and anti-Vietnam War
    movement, 146
Nonprofit corporation
  as organizational struc-
    ture, 76

responsibilities of Board of
    Directors of, 82–85
  tax status of, 78–79
Nonviolent action
  uses of, 40–42, 46–47n16
Norms
  for organizational com-
    munication, 177–178
North American Free
    Trade Agreement
    (NAFTA), 8
Norway
  social movements in, 16,
    26n3
NTL Institute, 208n10
Nuclear Freeze, 49
Nuclear power, 20, 24
Nurturing
  devaluation of, 44

Oka, Mohawk protest at,
    42
Oppenheimer, Martin, 40
Oppression
  internalized, 15–16, 144,
    151–152
  and leadership of social
    movements, 30–32
  ranking of, 170, 172n13
Organization
  stages of growth of, 58–63
Organization level
  of social change, 10
Organizing, 36
  and community, 42–44
  direct action and, 39
  neighborhood, 51–52
  resource-based, 32–34
*Organizing for Social
    Change* (Bobo, Ken-
    dall and Max), 35
Orientation
  supervision and, 134

Paul, Alice, 53
Peace Brigades Interna-
    tional
  use of nonviolent action
    by, 42
Peck, M. Scott, 43, 204
Philadelphia Inquirer, 40
Physical fitness
  as means of coping with
    stress, 197
Pittston Coal Company
  strike against, 47n.16
Planning, organizational,
    82–83
  effective process of, 112–
    113
  group mission and, 107–
    109
  group values and, 106–107
  information gathering
    and, 113–116
  resistance to, 109–112
Policies
  of nonprofit corporations,
    83–84
Political *vs.* personal
  and sustaining morale,
    144, 153–155
Politics
  connection between spiri-
    tuality and, 6
Power
  analysis of, 27–30, 39
  and fear of cooptation, 37
  handling of, 45
  and leadership, 31–32, 96
  See also Empowerment
Power-from-within, 29
  obstacles to, 42
Power-over, 27–30
Power-with, 29
  obstacles to, 42
Prejudice, diversity and,
    158–159

Primary system
    as first stage of activist or-
        ganization, 58–61
Problem-solving
    and empowerment, 34–35
    use of steering committees
        in, 102–105
Process goals
    in meetings, 118
Process observer, 124–125
Pseudocommunity level
    of community building,
        43, 44
Public image, 84
Public opinion
    and MAP, 17

Queer Nation, 152

Racism
    and organizational devel-
        opment of diversity, 169
Re-evaluation Counsel-
    ing, 33
    as means of coping with
        stress, 207
Reflective imaging
    as means of coping with
        stress, 206
Relaxation
    as means of coping with
        stress, 205–206
Resources, 32–34, 83
    and choosing Board of Di-
        rectors, 88
    supervision and, 134
    See also Funding
Risk, degree of
    role of, in trust-building,
        175, 176

Scarcity mentality, 33, 86,
    87, 204

Secondary system
    as second stage of activist
        organization, 61–63
Self-esteem
    internalized oppression
        and, 15–16
    overwork and, 196
Self-hypnosis
    as means of coping with
        stress, 205
Self-respect
    morale and, 147–151
Simonton, Stephanie, 198
Social change, 5
    levels of, 6–7, 10
    role of social movements
        in, 14–17
    See also Social movements
Social circles
    and recruitment for social
        movements, 49–55
Socialism, democratic, 8
Social movements, 7,
    26nn3
    development of, 10
    factors in, 6
    as impetus for social
        change, 14–17
    leadership in, 30–32, 34
    MAP and, 17–25
    organizing model vs. serv-
        ice model of, 35–36
    recruitment from social
        circles for, 49–55
    See also specific move-
        ments
Solidarity (Polish workers
    movement), 34
Southern Christian Lead-
    ership Conference, 6,
    17, 19
Spirituality
    connection between poli-
        tics and, 6

Starhawk
    analysis of power by, 27–30
Steering committee
    and problem-solving, 102–
        105
Stress
    means of coping with,
        196–207
    role of, in working for so-
        cial change, 195
Structure, organizational, 64
    forms of, 68–76
    incorporation and tax ex-
        emption and, 76–79
    membership and, 65–67
    role of, in coping with
        stress, 201–202
Student movement, 24
Students for a Democratic
    Society, 31
Suffrage movement, 53
Supervision, 134
    evaluation of, 138–141
    and feedback system, 135–
        137
    and organizational values,
        129–131
    role of, in coping with
        stress, 201–202
    supporting the relation-
        ship of, 141–143
    system of, 132–133
Support groups
    as means of coping with
        stress, 198–199
Sweden
    social movements in, 15

Tax exemption
    and organizational struc-
        ture, 76–79
Teams
    as element of organiza-
        tional structure, 71–74

Technology
influence of, on social
movements, 7
Therapy
as means of coping with
stress, 207
"The Tyranny of Struc-
turelessness" (Free-
man), 75
*Thinking Strategically: A
Primer on Long-
Range Strategic Plan -
ning* (Kehler, Ayvaz-
ian and Senturia), 113
Three Mile Island
stage four of MAP and, 20
Timekeeping
importance of, in meet-
ings, 122
Time management
as means of coping with
stress, 204
Trust
components of, 175–177

Unemployment
and capitalism, 14–15
United Farmworkers, 40,
46–47n16
use of house meetings by,
52
United Mineworkers of
America, 46–47n16
Ury, William, 190, 191
U.S. Democratic Party
and civil rights move-
ment, 38
U.S. Internal Revenue
Service (IRS)
and incorporation and tax
exemption, 78
U.S. Republican Party, 38

Vaill, Peter B., 12n1

Values
organizational planning
and, 106–107
supervision process and,
129–131
Vibes watcher. *See* Process observer
Vision statements
organizational planning
and, 109
Volunteers
as unpaid staff, 131–132

"Window of authority,"
97–99
Woman's Party, 53
Women's movement, 24
organizational structure
in, 75
self-esteem and, 15
Work plans
and supervision, 143

NEW SOCIETY PUBLISHERS

NEW SOCIETY PUBLISHERS is a not-for-profit, worker-controlled publishing house. We are proud to be the only publishing house in North America committed to fundamental social change through nonviolent action.

We are connected to a growing worldwide network of peace, feminist, religious, environmental, and human rights activists, of which we are an active part. We are proud to offer powerful nonviolent alternatives to the harsh and violent industrial and social systems in which we all participate. And we deeply appreciate that so many of you continue to look to us for resources in these challenging and promising times.

New Society Publishers is a project of the New Society Educational Foundation and the Catalyst Education Society. We are not the subsidiary of any transnational corporation; we are not beholden to any other organization; and we have neither stockholders nor owners in any traditional business sense. We hold this publishing house in trust for you, our readers and supporters, and we appreciate your contributions and feedback.

New Society Publishers
4527 Springfield Avenue
Philadelphia, Pennsylvania
19143

New Society Publishers
P.O. Box 189
Gabriola Island, British Columbia
V0R 1X0